CW00739701

From Fish To Colossus

How the German Lorenz Cipher was broken at Bletchley Park

Harvey G. Cragon

Cragon Books
8600 Skyline Dr. #1102
Dallas, Texas 75243

Second Edition

Manufactured in the United States

Bradley Graphics & Printing
Plano, Texas

ISBN 0-9743045-0-6

Front photograph: Figure 8.11
Back photograph: Figure 2.1

To Anthony Edgar Sale

Contents

Preface

In 1940 the German army began establishing a system of point-to-point teleprinter communication links between Hitler's headquarters and various Army and Army Group headquarters. Messages on these links were enciphered and deciphered by means of a machine designed and manufactured by C. Lorenz AG, a German manufacturer of various electronic and communications equipment. When the British Government Communications Headquarters (GCHQ) at Bletchley Park became aware of these links, the code name Fish was given to the system.

As specific links were identified, each was given a code name, such as Tunny (the first link identified), Octopus, Codfish, Squid, and Bream. These links were not in a network and each had its own keys and protocols. Thus, unlike the Enigma networks, each link had to be treated separately by Bletchley Park.

Fish ciphertext messages were in an additive cipher, unlike the substitution cipher of the Enigma. The Lorenz machine generated a pseudo random stream of characters that were added to the plaintext characters. Thus the system seemed to be a form of a One Time Pad that should have been unbreakable. However, William Tutte discovered that though the characters and single channels were pseudo random, the bits or channels taken two at a time were not pseudo random. This insight pointed the way to the routine breaking of Lorenz ciphertext.

After the initial break into Fish in 1941, GCHQ realized that the only feasible approach to breaking these messages in high volume was one based on the statistics of a single ciphertext message. Therefore, GCHQ conducted research into the required statistical analysis algorithms and the design and construction of machines required to perform statistical analysis on large volumes of data.

The machines designed and built to support the breaking of Fish messages were given names such as Heath Robinson, Colossus, Angel, and Junior, to name a few. This book concentrates on the machine aspects of the work at GCHQ. The cryptographic work, though important, is not as well documented and is not emphasized here.

The Government Code and Cipher School, GC&CS, was moved from London in August 1939 and renamed the Government Communications Headquarters GCHQ.[1] As the events described in this book occurred after 1939, the activity at Bletchley Park is referred to as occurring at GCHQ.

For most of the years after WWII information on Fish was sketchy. However, in 1996 the National Security Agency declassified approximately 1 million pages of documents dating back to World War 1. This information now resides at the National Archives and Records Administration in College Park, MD. A small group of these documents contain the information that is the primary resource for this book. Another document, released to the Public Record Office in 2000, by Michie, Good, and Timms, is another valuable source of information.

There are problems with using this information as the author(s) were writing under heavy security for readers who had significant backgrounds in the subject. Another problem is that no standard terminology had been established while the work was underway. Many of these documents are not dated and sometimes the author(s) is not identified. It is impossible to give a chronology with confidence that events are in the proper order and that accurate credit is given to the developer of a particular technique or equipment.

A second source of reference is books published in the last ten years that have sections devoted to Fish based on the recollections of the authors or interviews with participants at GCHQ. These accounts differ in some details as is common with oral history; judgments were made on my part as to the correct interpretation of events.

Beginning with introductory chapters on the development of the teletype and the Lorenz cipher machine, the events recounted in this book occurred over the period from mid 1940 to mid 1945, about five years. A chronology is given in Appendix A. The chronology should be kept in mind as the various techniques and equipment are discussed.

A reading guide to the book is given in the figure below. The flow of information in GCHQ is shown as a block diagram with the book chapters identified. The only topic not discussed is the translation of German plaintext into English.

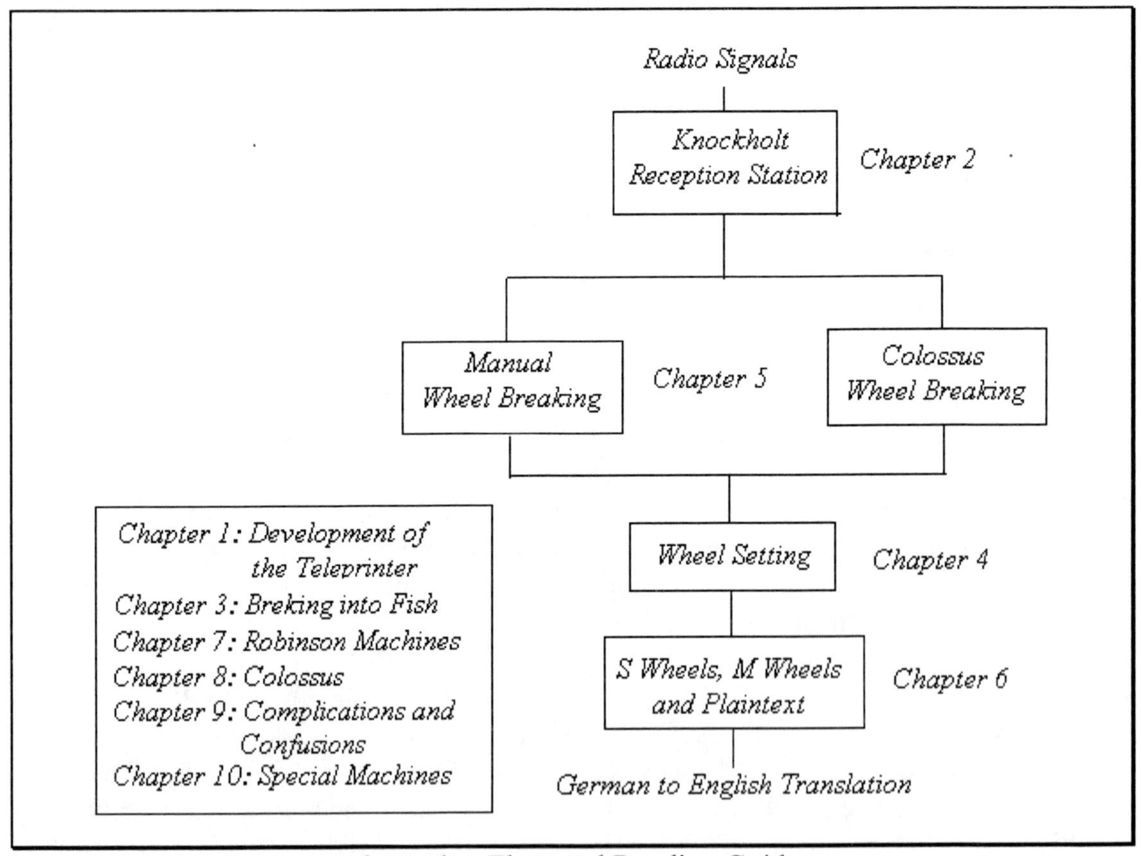

Information Flow and Reading Guide

One constant theme in this book is the dependence on statistical analysis rather than conventional code breaking. In his report of the cryptographic achievement at

GCHQ 1945, W. Jacobs, Technician 4th Grade, reported to Lt. Col. Frank Rowlett* in part:

> "The philosophical approach to the problem is modern in two respects. In the first place, it was recognized early that to study the system thoroughly, advanced mathematics was essential. Accordingly, men of wide mathematical, rather than wide cryptanalytic, background were employed. Secondly, it was essential, in dealing with the operational problem of such magnitude, to develop a means of spreading the solving effort widely, without stretching it too thin. The amount of material to be solved is so enormous that it is out of the question to get enough persons and equipment to work on all of it." [2]

Jacobs noted, "In March, 1945, upwards of five million letters of current transmission, containing intelligence of the highest order was deciphered." [3] At that time, the system at GCHQ described in this book had been up and running for about two years in a production basis. Thus approximately 7,000 characters were deciphered per day. Another indication of the productivity of GCHQ is given by Michie, Good, and Timms who write in reference to the section called the Testery, headed by Maj. Tester, "In May [1943] the section decoded over 1,400,000 letters, a figure which was not equaled until March, 1944, when the Newmanry was in full swing."[4]

They also report that the total number of characters decoded from November 1943 until the end of the war as 63,431,000. [5] This was truly a prodigious effort by a dedicated and talented group.

---

[1] Welchman, G., *The Hut Six Story*, McGraw-Hill Bock company, New York, pg. 10

[2] Jacobs, W. *The Chryptanalysis of the Tunny Cipher Device, Preface,* 1945, NARA, RG 457, Box 943, College Park, MD, pg. 1.

[3] (ibid., 1)

[4] Michie, D., Good, J., Timms, G.,*General Report on Tunny*, 1945, Released to the Public Record Office in 2000, http://www.alanturing.net/tunny_report, pg. 317.

[5] (ibid., 394).

---

* Col. Rowlett was in charge of the group that broke the Japanese Purple cipher and was a co-developer of the SIGBA cipher machine.

Acknowledgements

At the end of World War II, the cipher-breaking organizations at Bletchley Park were dismantled and most of the cipher-breaking machines were destroyed as well as their documentation. However, through the determined efforts of Tony Sale to gather surviving documentation, and to interview those designers still living, two cipher-breaking machines now are on display at Bletchley Park. The information Tony gathered enabled him and a group of volunteers to design and build working replicas of a Colossus and a Heath Robinson.

Because Tony Sale generously shared his information, including placing much of it on the Internet, this book has been made possible. This author is grateful for his personal assistance.

I am indebted to Bill Tutte of The University of Waterloo (Bill died in May 2002) and Frank Carter for their help in unraveling some of the issues of breaking into Fish and the development of the Colossus. In all cases, any errors in this book are the responsibility of the author, not the individuals who provided information.

Chapter 1

Development of the Teleprinter

Background

In the years between World War I and World War II, electrical and radio communications changed from the use of Morse code to the use of teleprinter machines.* The skill of the Morse telegrapher was replaced by teleprinters that automatically converted keyboard depressions into coded signals for transmission. At the receiving end, a similar teleprinter machine automatically interpreted the coded signals and printed the text.

Samuel Morse is credited with the invention of the telegraph as we know it today. There were many competing ideas for "electric communications" in both the U.S. and in Europe. However, the Morse system of transmission, a simple sending and receiving apparatus, and a code to represents symbols achieved overwhelming acceptance worldwide.

Because the Morse system required highly skilled operators both for sending and receiving messages, a labor aristocracy developed who enjoyed high esteem and high pay. Expert telegraphers could travel and live anywhere and be assured of finding instant employment. At the same time, telegraph inventors searched for an apparatus that would eliminate the need for skilled operators and make the telegraph more user friendly. These devices included such things as, automatic receivers that printed the incoming message and automatic transmitters that rapidly transmitted a message, which had been previously punched into paper tape. When these two apparatuses were combined with a keyboard and a printer, the first teleprinter appeared in the early 20th century.

With a teleprinter, an operator sends a message by typing the text on a standard keyboard while punching a paper tape. The paper tape is then read by a reader machine that transmits the message to the receiving station where another paper tape is punched. This tape is then read by the teleprinter and the message is typed. Only the skill of typing and handling the simple procedures associated with the paper tape are required.

Teleprinters were first applied on landline communication paths. As radio technology improved, radio paths were used. Today instant messaging over the Internet uses landline, fiber optic cables, microwave radio and satellites.

Teleprinters found wide application in business, the military and the diplomatic services. Starting in the 1920's, the code used between teleprinters was named the Baudot code after its developer Emile Baudot in 1874. We find the shadow of the Baudot code in the common ASCII code use with modern computer and in Internet messaging.

During World War I, teleprinters were used between higher headquarters by both the Allies and the Central Powers using landlines. The bulk and weight of the required equipment restricted the use of teleprinters so encoded and enciphered Morse radio communications and telephone messaging were used between lower headquarters.

---

* Known in the U.S. as Teletype machines, the name given by the Bell System.

The Baudot Code

The code used with teleprinters is called either the Baudot Code or the International Teleprinter Code.* This code used a fixed number, five, of signs for each character as compared to Morse code, which uses a variable length code (one to six dot or dash signs) for each character. Over a landline two different voltages or two different current directions conveyed the signs.

Teleprinters communicate in one of two modes. First, the teleprinters are connected directly on-line to each other. Typing on one teleprinter results in almost immediate printing on the other. Second, a more common mode of operation is that the sending teleprinter punches a paper tape as the text is entered into the keyboard. The tape is read by a high speed tape reader attached to the transmission medium (wire or radio) and the message is sent. The receiving teleprinter punches a tape for later printing. This mode of operation more fully uses the bandwidth of the communications medium.

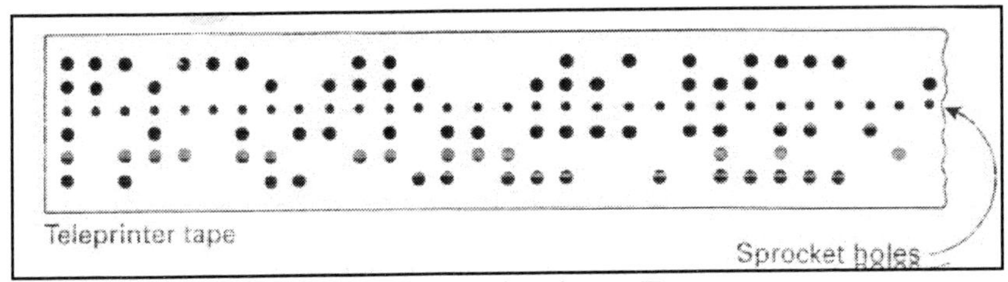

Figure 1.1 Teleprinter Tape
(Reprinted by Permission of Oxford University Press)

The Baudot code as it would be punched in a tape is shown in Figure 1.1. The black dots indicate where a hole is punched in the tape while a blank indicate no-punch. A central string of small holes are used to drive the tape by means of a sprocket.

The terminology used at Bletchley Park to describe the Baudot Code called a punch a "cross or X" and a no-punch a "dot or •". In this book the more common terminology is used that a punch is called a "one" or "1" and a no-punch is called a "zero" or "0". Thus X = 1 and • = 0.

The International Telegraph Alphabet No. 2 used by the Germans is shown in Tables 1.1 and 1.2.[1] With five bits, there are 32 unique codes available. Twenty-six of the codes are allocated to the letters of the alphabet, shown in Table 1.1

The allocation of functions to the six remaining codes is shown in Table 1.2. Because it is difficult to provide a concise abbreviation of these functions, various users have arbitrarily allocated single symbols to them such as the 8, 5, 4, 9, 3, and / of Table 1.2 are those used in *Report on the British Attack on Fish.*[†] [2]

---

* There are many variations of the International Teleprinter Code. The use of the term Baudot code is unfortunate as the International Teleprinter Code is based on the Murray code.

† The symbols 4, 3, and / were hidden by the teleprinter that created the message tape and never appear in plaintext.

Table 1.1, ITA-2 Letter and Figure Codes

Letters (LC)	Code	Figures (UC)
	12345	
A	11000	-
B	10011	?
C	01110	:
D	10010	Werde (Who)
E	10000	3
F	10110	%
G	01011	
H	00101	Currency
I	01100	8
J	11010	Bell
K	11110	(
L	01001	)
M	00111	. (Full Stop)
N	00110	,
O	00011	9
P	01101	0 (Zero)
Q	11101	1
R	01010	4
S	10100	‘
T	00001	5
U	11100	7
V	01111	=
W	11001	2
X	10111	/
Y	10101	6
Z	10001	+

Table 1.2 ITA-2 Control Codes

Code	Function	*Function Symbols*
12345		
11111	Go to Letters (LC)	8
11011	Go to Figures (UC)	5
01000	Line Feed	4
00100	Space	9
00010	Carriage Return	3
00000	Null, not used	/

Note that there are two codes, 11111 and 11011 that shift the meaning of the codes between Figures(UC) and Letters(LC), columns 1 and 3 of Table 1.1. This use of these codes is similar to the “caps lock” key on a personal computer keyboard. Also note that there are a number of codes that are given special local character meanings. For example, code 00101 is the code for the local currency. However, the code for the letters and numerals is fixed among all users.

The bits in the code are numbered from left to right, 1,2,3,4, and 5. In Figure 1.1, the bits are numbered top to bottom. These bits are sometimes shown in reverse order, as they would appear if the paper tape were viewed from the back.

Teleprinter Machines

Figure 1.2 shows a Lorenz T32Lo teleprinter from the period of 1936. This machine is typical of the teleprinters used by both sides in World War II. Note that the paper tape punch and reader are not integral to this machine. Also note there are 32 keys that correspond to the 32 codes of the Baudot system. If the markings on the keys were visible, they would be seen to follow the German version of the English QWERTY system: QWERTZ.

Figure 1.2 Teleprinter
(Courtesy Telemuseum)

By the mid-1930s, highly skilled telegraphers had been replaced by systems of teleprinters for most commercial and military communications.[3] Morse code over radio networks still dominated military applications where the size, weight, and cost of teleprinters forbade their use.* The famous Enigma system relied on Morse transmission, as did most in-flight operations by all nations. However, many countries adopted teleprinters for naval communications, except for the use of Morse code and Enigma cipher machines on German submarines.

Hellschreiber

One interesting side story in the development of non-Morse systems, which has relevance to the Colossus story, is the invention and use of a character-transmitting system invented by Dr. Rudolf Hell and patented in 1929.[4] The Hellschreiber was first used operationally by the German Condor Legion during the Spanish Civil War and was used in various forms by the German army throughout WWII. A Hellschreiber system operating over a radio link was used for the first experimental transmissions of Lorenz ciphertext in 1940. This use is briefly described in Chapter 3.

This device is a primitive form of facsimile which transmitted characters in an array of dots or pixels. The letters B, C, D, and E are shown in Figure 1.3. Each character is mapped into a 7×7 matrix, similar to many early matrix printers.[5]

* Voice radio and telephone were used extensively for tactical communications in World War II. These communications were given security by means of codes, not ciphers.

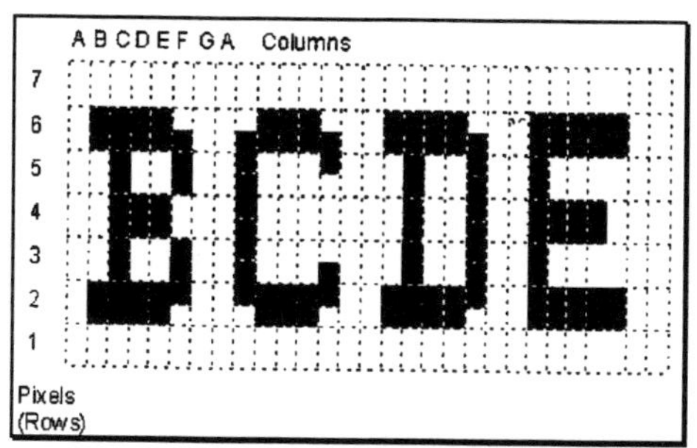

Figure 1.3 Hellschreiber Dot Matrix
(Courtesy Murray Greenman)

One implementation of the Hellschreiber is called "Feld-Hell." This machine had a rotating drum, shown in Figure 1.4, with 40 brass contact positions that generated the unique patterns for each of the 26 alphabetic characters, the decimal digits and other characters. When a character key was depressed, the drum rotated once, producing the pixel bit pattern for that character or symbol. Note that the keyboard layout is the German language version of the QWERTY format, Z and Y are interchanged.

Figure 1.4 Hellschreiber Keyboard and Drum
(Courtesy of Helge Fykse)

At the receiving end, a helical screw or worm shaft scanned a strip of paper. The edge of the helix was inked from an ink pad wheel. In response to the received pixels, a relay-engaged hammer hits the paper leaving an ink dot. A photograph of the printer is shown in Figure 1.5. The screw worm shaft can be seen but the hammer is not visible in this view.

Figure 1.5 Hellschreiber Printer Mechanism
(Courtesy of Helge Fykse)

Figure 1.6 shows another view of the Hellschreiber printer and a portion of the keyboard. An extensive set of photographs has been placed on the Internet by Helge Fykse. [6]

Figure 1.5 Hellschreiber Printer and Keyboard
(Courtesy of Helge Fykse)

References

[1] Michie, D., Good, J., Timms, G., *General Report on Tunny*, 1945, Public Record Office, Kew. Reference HW 25/4 and HW 25/5. Also http://www.alanturing.net/tunny_report/, pg.3.

[2] Anonymous, *Report on British Attack on "FISH"*, Communications Intelligence Technical Paper TS 47, Navy Department, Washington D.C., May 1945, NARA, RG 457, Box 607, Pg. 1.

[3] Standage, T., *The Victorian Internet*, Walker and Company, New York, 1998. Pg. 205.

[4] Greenman, M., http;//www.qsl.net/zl1bpu/FUZZY/Contents.html.

[5] Greenman, M., http://www.qsl.net/zl1bpu/FUZZY/Feld.html, pg. 1.

[6] http://www.laud.no/la6nca/radio/german/hell.htm.

Chapter 2

The Lorenz system

Background

At some time in the 1930s, the German Army worked with C. Lorenz AG to develop a security attachment for normal teleprinter communications. Teleprinter links were planned for very high level communications between Berlin and Army Headquarters. Because of the sensitive nature of these communications, the greatest possible security was required. The famous Enigma cipher system did not fit in well with a teleprinter environment with high volume point-to-point communications. It may also have been deemed not secure enough for this application. While the Lorenz system is generally considered to be used exclusively by the German Army, there is some evidence of limited naval use.[1]

Figure 2.1 shows a map of some of the Lorenz communications links. [2] These links were two-way, point-to-point, not networks where a number of stations shared the same frequencies and keys. Thus break-ins were more difficult than with the Enigma system where one goof by an Enigma originating operator could, and did, open up the complete network to break-in.

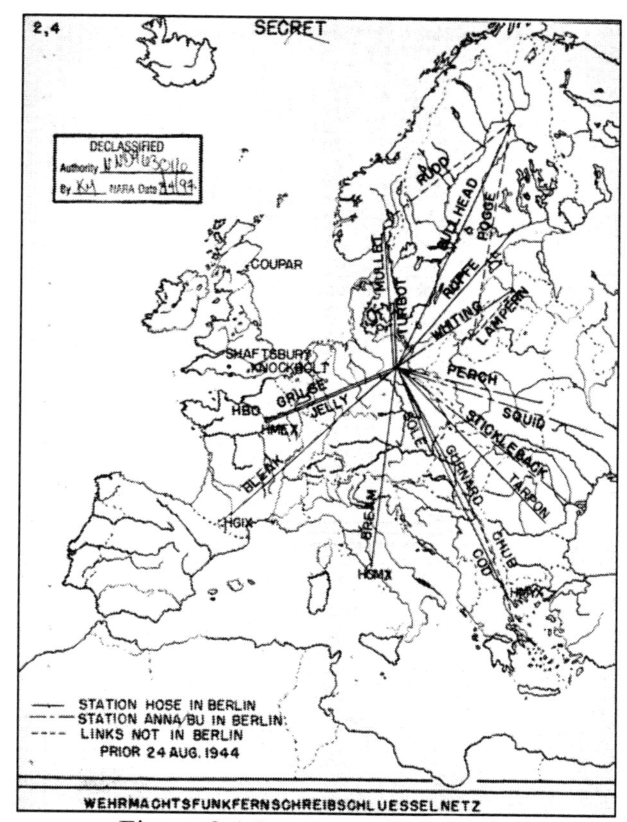

Figure 2.1 Lorenz or Fish Links

The number of Lorenz links increased rapidly from its introduction in 1942. In July 1943 there were six links, in autumn 1943 there were 10. In early 1944 the number of links increased to 26 and by the end of the war there were approximately 40 links. Each of these links used different keys and, in some cases, different operating procedures.[3] Note that the Lorenz system was not fully operational until just before the invasion of Europe in June 1944.

A Lorenz T32Lo teleprinter is shown in Figure 1.2 is typical of equipment used in the 1930s and 1940s. The security attachment was designed to be an addition to a teleprinter unlike the Enigma, which is a self-contained device.

Figure 2.2 shows the flow through the system when paper tape is used, that is, the sending and receiving teleprinters are not online. This mode was called Auto Mode at GCHQ. The plaintext is keyed into a teleprinter, creating a plaintext tape. This tape is read into the Lorenz machine, set up with key material. The ciphertext output is sent to the transmitter for radio or landline transmission. At the receiving end, the ciphertext is punched into a tape that is input to the Lorenz machine set up with the same key material. The output of the Lorenz is input to a teleprinter that produced the plaintext output. The ciphertext was never seen by either originating or receiving operators as there was no recording device between the two Lorenz machines.

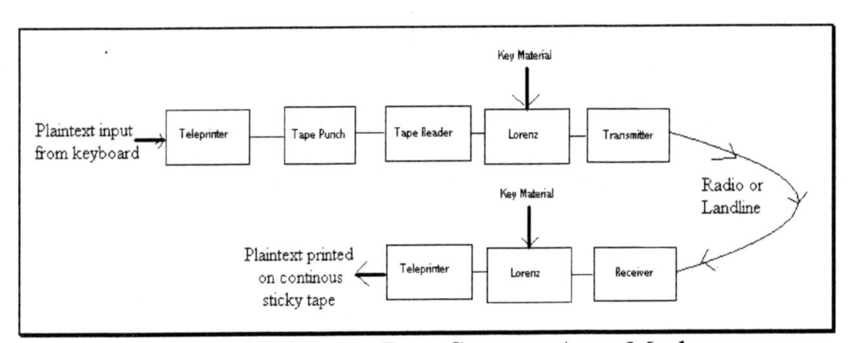

Figure 2.2 Lorenz Tape System, Auto Mode

The online operation of the Lorenz is shown in Figure 2.3, called Hand Mode at GCHQ. The plaintext is typed into the teleprinter; the plaintext is input to the Lorenz whose output is sent directly to the transmitter. The message is received, sent to the Lorenz and then to a teleprinter. This is the operating mode used for the famous message of August 30, 1941, described in Chapter 3.

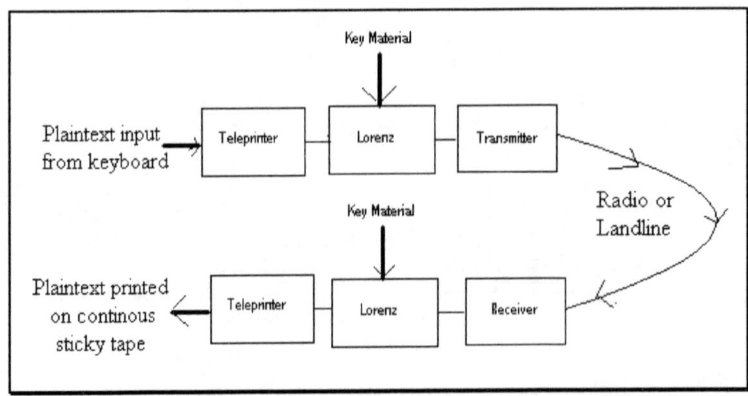

Figure 2.3 Lorenz Online System, Hand Mode

The Vernam Cipher System

The Lorenz encryption system, called Fish* by the British, was based on two U.S. patents.† The first (1,310,719) patent was issued to Gilbert S. Vernam in 1919 and assigned to the American Telephone and Telegraph Company, by whom Vernam was employed, Figure 2.4. AT&T engineers were working on ideas for securing teleprinter links for both commercial and military applications when Vernam invented this cipher system and obtained this patent.

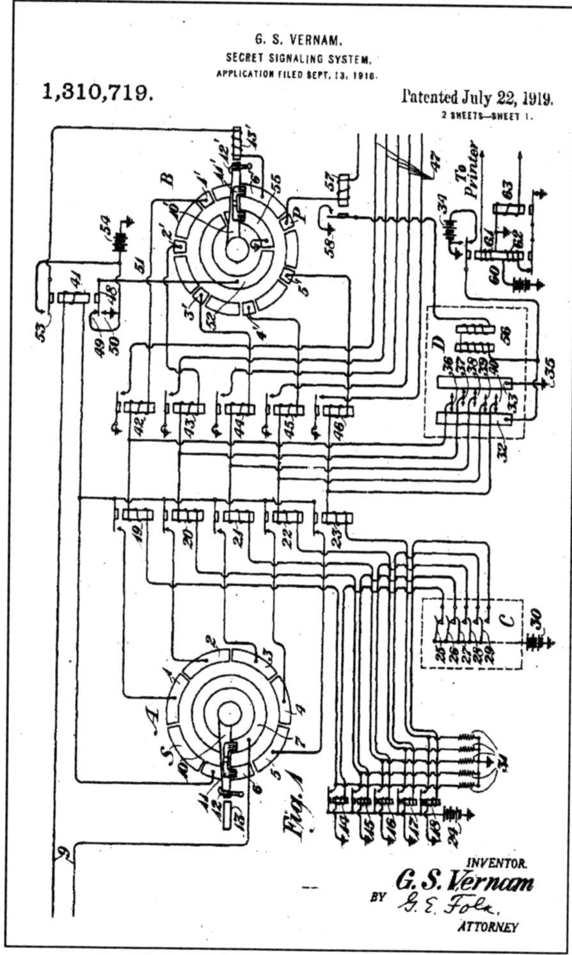

Figure 2.4 Vernam Patent

Vernam's invention mixed the plaintext Baudot-coded output of a teleprinter with a key tape, punched with a random sequence of characters in teleprinter code. The area *D* in Figure 2.4 shows the reader for the key tape and the area *C* shows the plaintext keyboard switches. The mixing was to be accomplished by modulo 2 addition, also called mod2 addition and non-carrying addition, by means of the ten relays shown in the center of the figure.

---

* Also called Tunny after the name given to the first broken link.

† The Lorenz cipher machine should not be confused with the German blind landing receivers also made by C. Lorenz AG used for directed bombing of England.

After the mod2 addition, the sending relays 14-18 sends the ciphertext character out to the receiving station. At the receiving teleprinter, an identical copy of the key tape is added mod2 to the ciphertext input stream of characters producing the Baudot codes of the plaintext. The key tape would have at least as many characters as the number of plaintext characters. If not, portions of the key would be reused and provide a skilled cryptanalyst an opening of depth * to recover the key.

Mod2 Addition

Mod2 addition has interesting properties; the rules for addition and subtraction are shown below. This function has the property that additions and subtractions are identical. Mod2 addition is also known as the "exclusive or", Xor, and by the symbol ⊕.

Mod2 Addition	Mod 2 Subtraction
0 + 0 = 0	0 - 0 = 0
1 + 0 = 1	1 - 0 = 1
0 + 1 = 1	0 - 1 = 1
1 + 1 = 0	1 - 1 = 0

As an example of the Vernam technique consider the plaintext message CALL and the Key ZBFC. The Baudot code, described in Tables 1.1 and 1.2, is used. The resulting cipher message is:

	C	A	L	L
Plaintext	01110	11000	01001	01001
⊕Key	10001	10011	10110	01110
Ciphertext	11111	01011	11111	00111
Ciphertext	letters	S	letters	M

The receiving teleprinter adds (or subtracts), mod2, the same key to the incoming ciphertext stream yielding the original plaintext message. This system in which the same key enciphers and deciphers is known as a "two way function" cipher.

	letters	S	letters	M
Ciphertext	11111	01011	11111	00111
⊕Key	10001	10011	10110	01110
Plaintext	01110	11000	01001	01001
Plaintext	C	A	L	L

The Morehouse Patent

Vernam envisioned a very long key tape that was in essence a one-time pad (OTP), the only known theoretically unbreakable cipher system. G. S. Vernam, L. F. Morehouse and J. O. Mauborgne, (Chief Signal Officer, U.S. Army) are generally given credit for devising the OTP.[4] However, the logistics of managing very long OTP tapes in a military environment were daunting. Subsequently, L. F. Morehouse patented the idea that two short key tapes could be used instead of one long tape. This patent, 1,356,546, also assigned to AT&T, is shown in Figure 2.5. The characters of the two key tapes are

* See Appendix C for a discussion of depth.

read by tape readers *X* and *Y* and are added mod2 to yield another key, KeyC.* The plaintext tape is read by reader *A* and added mod2 to KeyC to produce the ciphertext character stream. Actually, these three streams, KeyX, KeyY and *A* are added together in one step by the relays in the center of the first page of the Morehouse patent, Figure 2.5. The process is repeated at the receiving end to produce the plaintext.

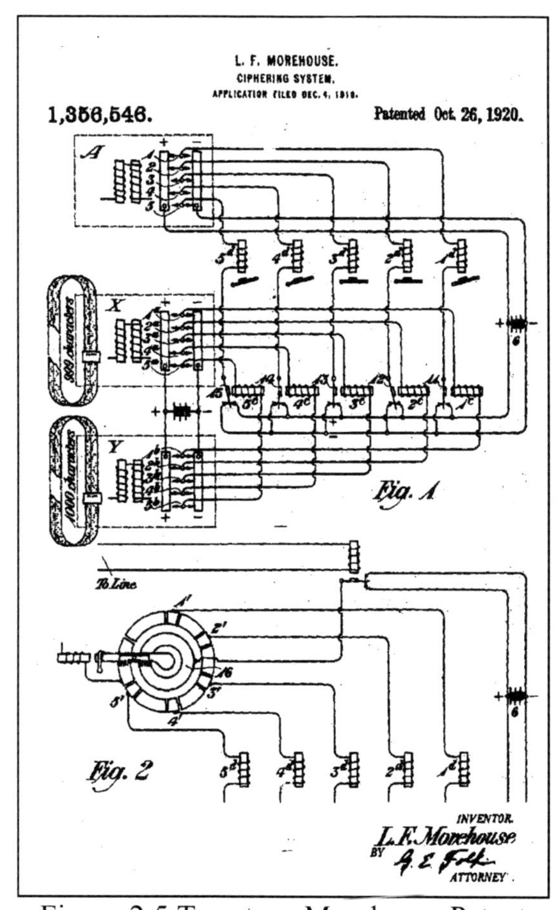

Figure 2.5 Two-tape Morehouse Patent

The motivation for this invention was to reduce the length of a single key tape. In the Morehouse patent, the concept of the two tapes having different lengths is described. The lengths of the two tapes, measured in characters, are relatively prime.† Morehouse suggested one tape of 999 characters the other of 1,000 characters. Because the lengths are relatively prime, the total length of the key will be 999,000 characters. Teleprinter tape is punched at about 10 characters per inch. Thus a 999,000-character tape would be about 8,325 feet long. Each of the two tapes of the Morehouse system would be about 8 1/2 feet in length, a more manageable system

The operation of Morehouse's patent is illustrated with the example used above. Four characters of KeyX (from tape 1) are ZBFC and four characters of YeyY (tape 2) are PRNQ; these two keys when added together give KeyC. Note that the three tapes can

* KeyC, the composite key, is referred to in Chapter 5 with the symbol *K*.

† Two integers are relatively prime if they share no common divisor except 1.

be added in one step, as illustrated in the patent, it is not necessary to have a two step process, which is shown below for clarity.

	Z	B	F	C
KeyX	10001	10011	10110	01110
	P	R	N	Q
⊕ KeyY	01101	01010	00110	11101
KeyC	11100	11001	10000	10011
	C	A	L	L
⊕ Plaintext	01110	11000	01001	01001
Ciphertext	10010	00001	11001	11010
Ciphertext	D	T	W	J

The receiving operator deciphers the message with identical copies of the two key tapes. The key tapes X and Y are added together to give KeyC. The ciphertext is added to KeyC to give the plaintext.

KeyX	10001	10011	10110	01110
⊕ KeyY	01101	01010	00110	11101
KeyC	11100	11001	10000	10011
⊕ Ciphertext	10010	00001	11001	11010
Plaintext	01110	11000	01001	01001
Plaintext	C	A	L	L

The fact that these two key tapes were combined to give KeyC does not significantly complicate the deciphering process. The long and the short tapes stepped together; thus the first 999 characters of the plaintext were enciphered with a first key. The second 999 characters were enciphered with a second key and so on.

W.F. Friedman devised and demonstrated in 1931 an attack on a Signal Corps system similar to the Vernam-Morehouse and the Lorenz cipher machines. The approach taken used cribs that were known endings of Department of State messages.* With a correct crib, two characters of the key could be identified and then the complete key.[5] This work is described in Appendix B.†

The Lorenz Cipher System

It seems that the engineers at Lorenz were aware of the Vernam and Morehouse patents. However, they believed that the management of one-time pad tapes (either one or two tapes) presented an impossible logistics problem even for communications between Hitler and his senior commanders. Thus they devised a mechanism that would generate, on the fly, the equivalent of a one-time pad. The sequence was fixed by setting 501 pins on twelve rotor wheels, described later in this chapter. This key sequence would not be random but pseudo-random, as it would repeat eventually. The length of the sequence before repeating was about 1.6×10^{19} characters. In comparison, the Enigma repeated after 17,576 characters for any one set of 3 wheels.

* A crib is a possible or probable word in the plaintext.

† In 1931, the U.S. Army purchased a ten pin-wheel machine from ITT that had been designed by Parker Hitt. Messages enciphered by this machine were broken in short order by the Army Signal Intelligence Service under the direction of William Friedman. See Appendix B.

The German reluctance to distribute one time pad tapes seems strange in retrospect. The monthly pin settings were distributed by courier, so why not tapes? Any number of multi-tape systems can be postulated that would have the same period of the Lorenz machine. However, there were a few incidents when the Germans transmitted the next month's wheel patterns enciphered by Lorenz.*

The Lorenz machine was called *Schlusselzusatz* or "Cipher attachment" and is shown in Fig. 2.6.[6] Note that the Lorenz has 12 wheels, called pinwheels.† Three versions of this machine were produced, the SZ 40, SZ 42A and the SZ 42B. The SZ 40 had no limitations, the SZ 42A and SZ 42B were introduced in 1942 with limitations.[7] The function of Limitations will be deferred until Chapter 9.

Figure 2.6 Lorenz Cipher Machine
(Reprinted by permission of Oxford University Press)

The rotational position of each wheel is indicated by a series of numbers on the face of the wheel. As will be discussed in Chapter 3, the starting positions of the wheels were conveyed in an alphabetic indicator; thus there must have been a mental conversion from alphabetical to numerical characters.

The Lorenz SZ40 and SZ42 should not be confused with a cipher machine made by Siemens and Halske. This machine, the T52 *Geheimschreiber* (Secret Writer) was a self-contained unit, not an attachment. The British in North Africa captured examples of the T52, and Arne Beurling broke the cipher in 1940 in Sweden. A description of this machine called "Sturgeon" and information on the work at GCHQ on breaking its cipher is available.[8 9]

---

* The Japanese, on occasion, distributed Purple key material via the Purple system because they had no secure transportation available for key distribution.

† The Enigma had three wheels; the naval Enigma had four wheels.

The operation of pinwheels is described in Figure 2.7 that shows two eight-position pinwheels. The setting positions of both wheels are at the index A. The left wheel produces the pattern 1 1 1 1 1 1 1 1 as it rotates while the right wheel produces the pattern 0 1 0 1 1 0 0 1 (when it starts at the A index position). The Design of the Lorenz wheels actually used a pin or slider that was set to be flush or to protrude from the face of the wheel. These pins engaged switches that generated the patterns of ones and zeros.

The pins on the Lorenz machine were lugs or the rim of the wheels that were slid between the operative and non-operative position, also shown in Figure 2.7

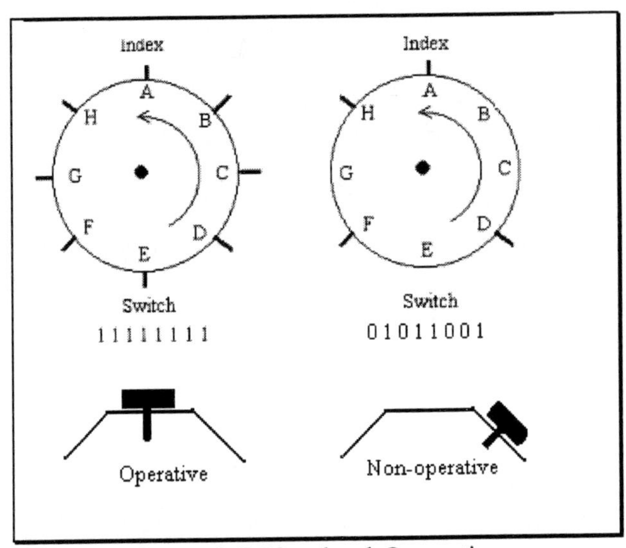

Figure 2.7 Pinwheel Operation

The operation and use of the wheels is shown in Figure 2.8. The Chi (called X) wheels and the M1 wheel step on each character enciphered or deciphered. The Psi (called S) wheels step in response to the pin settings of the M1 and M2 wheels. The plaintext input character stream enters from the left from either a teleprinters keyboard or a paper tape reader or, when it is the receiving system, from the radio receiver. The five individual Baudot code bits are added mod2 to the X and S wheels and then sent to the output on the right. The five output channels are sent over a landline or a radio channel or are connected to a teleprinter when it is the receiving system. These connections are shown in Figure3 2.2 and 2.3.

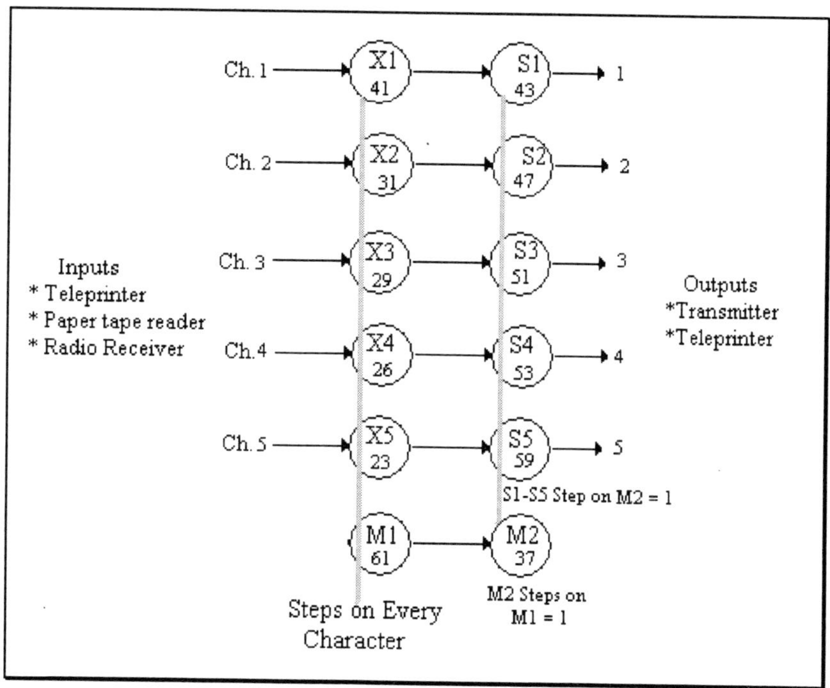

Figure 2.8 Lorenz Schematic

Message security

Message security was provided by two means. First, the wheels of the Lorenz cipher machine are pinwheels that produced a string of ones and zeros. The pattern of the pins (in or out) was changed on a periodic basis as instructed from a key distribution center. This is unlike the Enigma wheels that provided jumbled electrical connections giving a fixed substitution cipher or permutation.

Second, the setting or the initial rotational positions of the wheels were changed for each message, the wheel settings being conveyed in the message to the receiving operator.

Wheel Pin Patterns

The first level of security was provided by having the pin patterns of the wheels programmable by moving the pins to give a "one" or "zero" in each position. The wheel pattern was the first part of the key and that was distributed to the two stations on each link by courier. Because the Lorenz was used primarily for high level Army communications, the likelihood of the capture of documents describing the wheel patterns was remote, unlike the deployment of the Naval Enigma on submarines.

At the peak use, there were 40 or more Lorenz links and 80 machines in use at one time.[10] However, a backup machine accompanied each machine thus doubling the number of machines in use.[*] The periods for changing the wheel pin patterns are discussed in Chapters 3 and 9. There is no published information on whether or not wheel pin pattern documents were captured from the Germans either during or after the war.

---

[*] We can guess that no more than 250 Lorenz machines were produced, a number far smaller than the approximately 30,000 Enigmas.

Figure 2.7 shows a wheel with eight pin positions. However, the number of pin positions on the twelve wheels of Lorenz was discovered at Bletchley Park by cryptographic means, discussed in Chapter 3.The number of pins of Lorenz are shown in Figure 2.8 and repeated below. Note that Figure 2.8 uses the symbol K to denote a wheel, the symbol *X* is used in this book.

*X*1	41	*S*1	43	*M*1	61
*X*2	31	*S*2	47	*M*2	37
*X*3	29	*S*3	51		
*X*4	26	*S*4	53		
*X*5	23	*S*5	59.		

The numbers of wheel pin positions are all relatively prime numbers having no common factors. The reason for this design is to lengthen the sequence before a repeat. For practical reasons, discussed later, the number of setting positions was less than the length of the key cycle of 1.6×10^{19}.[*]

Determining the number of positions of each wheel was a major accomplishment in cryptanalysis at GCHQ. Only late in 1945 was a captured Lorenz made available for inspection. Upon inspecting this machine, they knew they had correctly fathomed its design.[†] Analogues of the Lorenz machine were constructed and used to decipher messages. These machines, called Tunny, are described in Chapter 10.

The number of pins to be positioned for a pattern is the sum of the number of pins on the twelve wheels: 501. Thus the number of unique wheel patterns is $2^{501} \div (1.6 \times 10^{19}) = 4 \times 10^{131}$. The divisor recognizes that some of the unique patterns are not valid and "a rotation of a pattern is the same pattern as far as the wheel-breaker is concerned."[11] For example, if all of the pins are set to "zero", the ciphertext is identical to the plaintext. The Germans did not rely completely on this large number of unique pin patterns to defeat any attempt at cracking the Lorenz system. The patterns of the pins were carefully designed as well, a topic covered in Chapter 9.

Wheel Setting Positions

The second level of security was provided by using the starting positions of the wheels as the message indicator (similar to the Enigma three letter indicator). The starting position, called the "wheel setting" at GCHQ, was selected by the originating operator and was not to be repeated for another message. Initially, the setting position indicator was communicated to the receiver in plaintext. The receiving operator set his machine to the same wheel setting positions and received the incoming message. The GCHQ called the process of finding the wheel setting of a ciphertext message *Wheel Setting* as well, a topic discussed in Chapter 4.

An examination of Figure 2.6 will show twelve setting rings. Five of these rings set the setting position of five wheels (the *X* wheels) that are equivalent to one of the Morehouse tapes. Another five rings set the wheel setting of the *S* rings that are

---

[*] 1.6×10^{19} is the product of the number of pins of the twelve wheels. That is, $41 \times 31 \times ... \times 37$.

[†] This is unlike the situation with the Enigma, which had been sold commercially; the only design unknowns were the rotor wiring and the steckerboard (plugboard).

equivalent to the second Morehouse tape. The other two rings set the wheel setting of the last two wheels (the *M1* and *M2* wheels) that control the stepping of the *S* wheels.

The setting wheels have alphabetic indicators. However, one photograph of a SZ42 shows numerals to establish the setting positions.[12] Only 25 letters of the alphabet are used (J is omitted) on eleven wheels while X_5 with only 23 setting positions has only 23 letters. Thus the total number of setting positions is: $25^{11} \times 23 \approx 5.4 \times 10^{16}$, only a small fraction of the 1.6×10^{19} possible setting positions. The equivalent number of Enigma setting positions is 17,576.

The indicator used in the early days consisted of twelve letters such as HQIBPEXEZMUG. In October 1942, the Germans replaced the twelve-character indicator with a Q code. A message sent in the clear would be of the form QEP32.* The number 32 indicated the entry on a previously agreed upon page of a codebook. The 32nd entry would be either a 12-character indicator or a numerical indicator for the ZS42 machines.[13]

The operating procedure for Lorenz was to change the *X* wheel patterns once a month, the *S* patterns every 3 months and the *M* wheel patterns every day. Starting in May 1942 the *S* patterns were changed on the first of each month.[14] A unique wheel setting for each message was chosen at random by the originating operator. Starting in the summer of 1944, the *X* and *S* wheel pin patterns were changed daily.† [15] The change schedule is further described in Chapter 9.

Message Format, Early Period

Ciphertext messages sent on the Lorenz system in the June-July 1941 period were probably messages to test the overall working of the system using standard teleprinters. The Hellschreiber had been abandoned by this time. These messages consisted of five components. [16]

1. The message serial number in plaintext repeated several times. Numbers were transmitted in alphabetic characters using a simple substitution 1 = Q, 2 = W, 3 = R, etc.

2. The message indicator revealing the twelve wheels setting positions were transmitted next using a spelled out phonetic alphabet such as Anton, Bertha, etc. The separators between names were Spaces called 9s (00100). Thus the message indicator was Anton9Bertha9, etc

3. Five Spaces, 00100.

4. The ciphertext.

5. A sequence of Go to Letters (11111). Called 8s.

---

* Q codes are used worldwide by radio operators for exchanging procedural information.

† As will be discussed in Chapter 8, this change increased the workload at GCHQ giving higher priority to the development, improvement, and production of Colossi.

The message format described above was the format in use early in the deployment of Lorenz by the Germans. A number of changes both to the placement of the message serial number and the method of designating the indicators were changed to confound the GC&SC. These changes are described in Chapter 9.

System Security

In addition to the security of the wheel patterns and wheel settings, additional security was provided in a set of operation rules. A report dated 26 Sept. 1944 by a special committee on cipher security gave the following rules.[17 18]

1. The SZ/40 and SZ/42 may be put in operation only on wire links
2. Each link is furnished with different keys
3. Keys are changed daily
4. Message length is limited to 10,000 characters

Rule #1must not have been enforced as Knockholt continued to receive radio messages after the date of this directive. Radio transmissions continued up to the fall of Germany

Rule #4 was not followed as much longer messages were processed at the GCHQ. These very long messages were usually a collection of short messages combined into one. The key was allowed to run as the messages were sent. See Appendix B for another example of the practice of combining messages to be sent with one key.

References

[1] Erskine, R. "From the Archives Tunny Decrypts" *Cryptologia,* Vol. XII, No. 1, January 1988, pg. 59-61.
[2] Anonymous, *Report on British Attack on "FISH",* Communications Intelligence Technical Paper TS 47, Navy Department, Washington D.C., May 1945, NARA RG 457, Box 607, pg. 16.
[3] Hinsley, F. H., "An Introduction to Fish". *Codebreakers, The Inside Story of Bletchley Park,* Ed. Hinsley, F. H., Stripp, A. Oxford University Press, 1993, pg. 142.
[4] Kahn, D. *The Codebreakers,* pg. 397-398.
[5] Rowlett, F. B., *The Story of Magic,* Aegean Park Press, 1998, pg. 66.
[6] Davies, D.W., "The Lorenz Cipher Machine SZ42", *Cryptologia,* Vol. XIX, No. 1, January 1995, pp. 39-61.
[7] Michie, D., Good, J., Timms, G., *General Report on Tunny,* 1945, Released to the Public Record Office in 2000, http://www.alanturing.net/tunny_report/, pg. 10.
[8] (Anonymous, *Report,* 7-11).
[9] Small, A. *Special Fish Report,* NARA, NR 4628 Box 1417, also http://www.codesandciphter.org.uk/documents/small/page112.htm, December 1944, pg. 76.
[10] (Anonymous, *Report,* 15).
[11] Good, J., "Enigma and Fish", *Codebreakers, The Inside Story of Bletchley Park,* Ed. Hinsley, F. H., Stripp, A. Oxford University Press,1993, pg. 153.
[12] (Davies, Lorenz Cipher Machine, 41).
[13] (Anonymous, *Report,* 14).
[14] (Michie, *General Report,* 308).
[15] (ibid., 319).
[16] (ibid, 297).
[17] Heider, Franz-Peter, Á Colossal Fish", *Cryptologia,* Vol. XXII, No. 1, January 1998, pp. 69-95.
[18] (ibid., 69-95).

Chapter 3

Breaking into Fish

Background

In the summer of 1940, a team searching for clandestine German radio transmitters in England heard strange radio signals. These radio signals were not in Morse code and were identified as Hellschreiber transmissions, an early form of FAX dating from the 1930's.[1] Some of these Hellschreiber signals were Lorenz ciphertext that were transmitted for testing the system and were discontinued in February 1941.[2]

Other signals, probably test transmissions, were received in May 1941 and were recognized as non-Hellschreiber and non-Morse signals. The signals did not originate in the UK; they were coming from German controlled Europe. Ultimately, in the Middle of 1941, the signals were identified as teleprinter messages between Athens and Vienna, a link named Tunny.[3] Some of the test messages were in plaintext prior to the use of the Lorenz system.

Breaking into the Fish System

By summer 1941, GCHQ personnel had learned a great deal about these mysterious signals. As teleprinter signals were well known, there was the problem of identifying the 26-letter codes and the 6-control codes which were employed, shown in Table 1.1 and Table 1.2.

It was immediately realized that only 16 characters were being received, not the 32 characters of a Baudot code, because the leading bit, Bit 1, was always a zero on a plaintext test message. It was assumed that Bit 1 was faulty (always sending a zero, never a one) on the German equipment during tests shortly after the German invasion of Russia on June 22, 1941.[4]

The enciphered message was preceded by a plaintext list of 12 names, HEINRICH, BERTHA, THEODOR, etc. These seemed to be an indicator having the letters: H, B, T...etc. The fault in bit one, HEINRICH was received as H(00000)INRICH while THEODOR was received as TH(00000)O(00010)OR. E and (00000) differ only in the first bit (10000 vs. 00000) while D and (00010) differ only in the first bit (10010 vs. 00010). This insight lead to the discovery that the 26 alphabetic characters were transmitted in international standard Baudot codes

After the allocation of the 26 alphabetic codes was established, this left the question of the control characters to be discovered. By reasoning similar to that above, all of the control characters and their functions were settled.

Once the Germans stopped sending the plaintext test messages, the character of the messages changed and it was obvious the messages were enciphered in some way.

The problem then was to decide on the type of cipher being used, to find a way to recover the plaintext, and to discover the design of the cipher machine. By accomplishing these ends, procedures could be established and equipment could be designed and produced to break these cipher messages on a routine basis as was being done with Enigma messages.

The GCHQ cryptanalysts knew a great deal. They were aware of the Vernam and Morehouse patents. They also knew of pinwheel cipher machines, such as the Parker Hitt machine discussed in Appendix B, and they deduced from the 12 indicator letters that the machine used by the Germans had two banks of five wheels each. By elimination, they deduced that the other two indicator letters would, in some way, influence the stepping of the ten wheels. The plaintext would be added mod2 to the two banks of five wheels to produce the ciphertext, just as in the Morehouse patent. They also deduced that the indicator letters would refer to the starting positions of 12 devices that produce the streams of ones and zeros composing the key. They correctly found that mod2 addition was used as described in the Vernam and Morehouse patents. However, they still had a long way to go to find the design of the machine and its keying method.

In April, May, and June, a staff was assembled at GCHQ* to deal with Fish but little progress was made in recovering the organization of the machine or the keys other than the indicators. Then, on August 30, 1941 a German operator provided the vital clues that unzipped the entire system.† [5]

The GCHQ had been looking for just such a mistake to be made. One powerful technique for recovering ciphers and codes is the use of "depth", discussed in Appendix C. Depth means that two or more messages are received that have overlapping use of all or a portion of a key. For GCHQ, the best of all worlds happened. The system was being operated in Hand mode rather than in Auto mode with tape and the same key was used to encipher essentially the same message.

The first message of approximately 4,000 characters was transmitted, and then the receiving operator signaled that the message was garbled and should be sent again. The originating and receiving operators reset their machine to the original wheel setting and retransmission was started. However, the originating operator must have been mad at himself for having to redo the work of typing the message and used abbreviations and had misspellings in some places. Thus two almost identical messages were enciphered with the same key. The first message started with SPRUCHNUMMER the second message started with SPRUCHNR.‡

Additive and Subtractive Ciphers

The cryptanalysts may have been aware of the work done by Friedman and his staff on the ITT additive ciphers in 1931, described in Appendix B.[6] In addition, Major Gerry Morgan§ had published an undated paper on letter subtractors.[7] This paper described a system using decimal addition where the characters were coded 1, 2, ...26.

Morgan's paper on letter-subtractor machines clearly established the principles for breaking into two messages that are enciphered with the same key. The principle is that when the same key is used to encipher two different messages with modulo arithmetic, if the two messages are subtracted, the remainder is the sum of the two-

* Bill Tutte and Jack Good joined in May 1941.

† The Germans may have noted this security breach and stopped using Fish for a few days. They tightened up their procedures as no more messages in depth were received for the balance of 1941.

‡ The message number was enciphered giving a powerful crib.

§ Major Morgan was head of the Research Section and was concerned with breaking ciphers produced by the Hagelin C-38, letter subtractor machine used by the Italian Navy.

plaintext messages. The theory is the same for any modulus of arithmetic: 26 or 2 as in the case of the Lorenz. Morgan's Research Section is given credit for much of the preliminary theory behind this class of cipher machine. [8]

The process of extracting the key from two messages enciphered with the same key is:

Plaintext 1 ⊕ Key = Ciphertext 1
Plaintext 2 ⊕ Key = Ciphertext 2.

Ciphertext 1 ⊕ Ciphertext 2 = (Plaintext 1 ⊕ Key) ⊕ (Plaintext 2 ⊕ Key)
= Plaintext 1 ⊕ Plaintext 2 ⊕ (Key ⊕ Key)[*]
= Plaintext 1 ⊕ Plaintext 2
= Φ.[†]

If the two plaintext messages can be untangled from the sum by cribs and anagramming, the key can be computed. This is accomplished by adding each of the plaintext to its corresponding ciphertext.

Key = Plaintext 1 ⊕ Ciphertext 1
Key = Plaintext 2 ⊕ Ciphertext 2

The technique used at GCHQ to recover the Key used in the message of August 30, 1941 will be illustrated. Assume two messages; Plaintext 1 is the message CALL and Plaintext 2 is the message HELP. The same key will be used to encipher both messages (U W E B).

	C	A	L	L	H	E	L	P
Plaintext	01110	11000	01001	01001	00101	10000	01001	01101
⊕Key	11100	11001	10000	10011	11100	11001	10000	10011
Ciphertext	10010	00001	11001	11010	11001	01001	11001	11110
Ciphertext	D	T	W	J	W	L	W	K

To start breaking this cipher, the two ciphertext messages are added together giving the sum of the plaintext characters, Φ.The Key character components have dropped out.

Ciphertext 1	10010	00001	11001	11010
⊕Ciphertext 2	11001	01001	11001	11110
= Φ	01011	01000	00000	00100
	G	(4) Line feed	/ (Null)	9 (Space)

This is all fine and good, but what two plaintext characters sum to 01011 or G? Further, what two plaintext letters sum to 4 (Line Feed), / (Null), and 9 (Space). Figure

[*] Recall that addition and subtraction are the same in mod2 arithmetic. Thus the two keys subtract and cancel.

[†] The sum of two ciphertext characters is called Φ.

3.1 shows the mod2 sums of the characters: one on the x and the other on the y-axis. The G of this example can be the sum of B,A or H,C or M,I etc. There are 16 pairs of characters or 32 combinations that sum to G. The question for the cryptanalyst is: which pair is the correct pair?

	A	B	C	D	E	F	G	H	I	J	K	L	M	N	O	P	Q	R	S	T	U	V	W	X	Y	Z	8	5	3	4	9	/
A	/	G	F	R	4	C	B	Q	S	3	N	Z	8	K	5	Y	H	D	I	W	9	X	T	V	P	L	M	O	J	E	U	A
B	G	/	Q	T	0	H	A	F	8	L	P	J	S	Y	E	K	C	W	M	D	V	U	R	9	N	3	I	4	Z	5	X	B
C	F	Q	/	U	K	A	H	G	3	S	E	M	L	4	P	O	B	9	J	V	D	T	X	W	5	8	Z	Y	I	N	R	C
D	R	T	U	/	3	9	W	X	K	4	I	5	Y	S	Z	8	V	A	N	B	C	Q	G	H	M	0	P	L	E	J	F	D
E	4	O	K	3	/	N	5	Y	U	R	C	W	X	F	B	Q	P	J	9	Z	I	8	L	M	H	T	V	G	D	A	S	E
F	C	H	A	9	N	/	Q	B	J	I	4	8	Z	E	Y	5	G	U	3	X	R	W	V	T	O	M	L	P	S	K	D	F
G	B	A	H	W	5	Q	/	C	M	Z	Y	3	I	P	4	N	F	T	8	R	X	9	D	U	K	J	S	E	L	O	V	G
H	Q	F	G	X	Y	B	C	/	L	8	5	I	3	0	N	4	A	V	Z	9	W	R	U	D	E	S	J	K	M	P	T	H
I	S	8	3	K	U	J	M	L	/	F	D	H	G	R	V	T	Z	N	A	P	E	O	Y	5	W	Q	B	X	C	9	4	I
J	3	L	S	4	R	I	Z	8	F	/	9	B	Q	U	W	X	M	E	C	5	N	Y	O	P	V	G	H	T	A	D	K	J
K	N	P	E	I	C	4	Y	5	D	9	/	X	W	A	Q	B	O	S	R	8	3	Z	M	L	G	V	T	5	U	F	J	K
L	Z	J	M	5	W	8	3	I	H	B	X	/	C	V	R	9	S	O	Q	4	Y	N	E	K	U	A	F	D	G	T	P	L
M	8	S	L	Y	X	Z	I	3	G	Q	W	C	/	T	9	R	J	P	B	N	5	4	K	E	D	F	A	U	H	V	O	M
N	K	Y	4	S	F	E	P	O	R	U	A	V	T	/	H	G	5	I	D	M	J	L	8	Z	B	X	W	V	9	C	4	N
O	5	E	P	Z	B	Y	4	N	V	W	Q	R	9	H	/	C	K	L	X	3	8	I	J	S	F	D	U	A	T	G	M	O
P	Y	K	O	8	Q	5	N	4	T	X	B	9	R	G	C	/	E	M	W	I	Z	3	S	J	A	U	D	F	V	H	L	P
Q	H	C	B	V	P	G	F	A	Z	M	O	S	J	5	K	E	/	X	L	U	T	D	9	R	4	I	3	N	8	Y	W	Q
R	D	W	9	A	J	U	T	V	N	E	S	O	P	I	L	M	X	/	K	G	F	H	B	Q	8	5	Y	Z	3	4	C	R
S	I	M	J	N	9	3	8	Z	A	C	R	Q	B	D	X	W	L	K	/	Y	4	5	P	O	T	H	G	V	D	U	E	S
T	W	D	V	B	Z	X	R	9	P	5	8	4	N	M	3	I	U	G	Y	/	Q	C	A	F	S	E	8	J	O	L	H	T
U	9	V	D	C	I	R	X	W	E	N	3	Y	5	J	8	Z	T	F	4	Q	/	B	H	G	L	P	O	M	K	S	A	U
V	X	U	T	Q	8	W	9	R	O	Y	Z	N	4	L	I	3	D	H	5	C	B	/	F	A	J	K	E	8	3	M	G	V
W	T	R	X	G	L	V	D	U	Y	O	M	E	K	8	J	S	9	B	P	A	H	F	/	C	I	4	N	3	5	Z	Q	W
X	V	9	W	H	M	T	U	D	5	P	L	K	E	Z	S	J	R	X	O	F	G	A	C	/	3	N	4	I	Y	8	B	X
Y	P	N	5	M	H	O	K	E	W	V	G	U	D	B	F	A	4	8	T	S	L	J	I	3	/	9	R	C	X	Y	B	Y
Z	L	4	8	O	T	M	J	S	Q	G	V	A	F	X	D	U	I	5	H	E	P	K	4	N	9	/	C	R	B	W	Y	Z
8	M	I	Z	P	V	L	S	J	B	H	T	F	A	W	U	D	3	Y	G	8	O	E	N	4	R	C	/	9	Q	X	5	8
5	O	4	Y	L	G	P	E	K	X	T	5	D	U	V	A	F	N	Z	V	J	M	8	3	I	C	R	9	/	W	B	8	5
3	J	Z	I	E	D	S	L	M	C	A	U	G	H	9	T	V	8	4	D	O	K	3	5	Y	X	B	Q	W	/	R	N	3
4	E	5	N	J	A	K	O	P	9	D	F	T	V	C	G	H	Y	3	U	L	S	M	Z	8	Y	W	X	B	R	/	I	4
9	U	X	R	F	S	D	V	T	4	K	J	P	O	3	M	L	W	C	E	H	A	G	Q	B	B	Y	5	8	N	I	/	9
/	A	B	C	D	E	F	G	H	I	J	K	L	M	N	O	P	Q	R	S	T	U	V	W	X	Y	Z	8	5	3	4	9	/

Figure 3.1 Mod2 Addition of Characters

We test the theory by adding the characters of the two plaintext words (CALL and HELP) and find that we get the character sequence G, 4, /, 9, when the two plaintext characters are added.

Plaintext 1	01110, C	11000, A	01001, L	01001, L
⊕ Plaintext 2	00101, H	10000, E	01001, L	01101, P
mod2 Sum	01011 G	01000 4 (Line Feed)	00000 / (Null)	00100 9 (Space)

Because this is a contrived example, we know the plaintext for the first characters are the pair (H, C). We do not know, however, which letter belongs to which plaintext. * A combination of cribbing and anagramming found the final plaintext, CALL and HELP.

Finding a crib and anagramming the two plaintext messages to give the correct sum are the most critical and difficult steps. This process is discussed further in the next section. Due to the difficulty of finding a crib and anagramming, a special purpose machine was built at GCHQ to perform the anagramming function. This machine, called "Proteus", is described in Chapter 10.[9]

Finding the Key

Col. Tiltman,† Figure 3.2[10], an experienced cryptanalyst (probably the best in England at the time, some say)[11], attacked the two messages received on August 30, 1941. Both messages had the same indicators, HQIBPEXEZMUG, and Col. Tiltman assumed, correctly, that the plaintext and key could be found by the method described above. He formed the sum of the ciphertext messages to remove the key and then untangled the sum of the two plaintexts. Viewed in the abstract, the problem of untangling the plaintext is a very large anagramming task. However, Tiltman found that he had two almost identical messages that could be "cribbed" to get started.

Figure 3.2 Col. John Tiltman

The first nine characters following the plaintext indicators were added giving eight nulls followed by F:

////////F. ‡ §

---

* Notice that for this example, the first letter of the two plain messages are not the same, C and H. Looking down the diagonal of Figure 3.1 from A,A to /,/ we see that the character G does not occur. Thus the first characters are not the same. In fact, adding a letter to itself always gives 00000 or /. The person breaking this cipher must have some additional information, such as a crib, to successfully untangle the plaintexts.

† Later promoted to Brigadier

‡ The Germans were enciphering the message serial number at this time.

§ Two identical characters when added mod2 will give / as shown in Figure 3.1

Therefore, the first eight characters of the two plaintexts were identical. For a crib, Col. Tiltman assumed that both messages started with the word "serialnumber" or *SPRUCHNUMMER* in German. The first eight characters of serial number are *SPRUCHN.* After eight characters the characters diverged with the sum character F. Under the assumption that *SPRUNCHNR* was an abbreviation of *SPRUCHNUMMER*, the characters R and U would sum to F. By these steps, the first nine characters of the key were found.*

By alternating between the two messages, and after several weeks of work, Col. Tiltman finally decomposed the sum of two-ciphertext messages into the two-plaintext messages themselves.† Now that Col. Tiltman had recovered both the plaintext and the ciphertext for both messages, all he had to do was to add Plaintext to Ciphertext and he had the key for the two messages.‡

However, if the two messages had been identical, as would have been the case if the messages had been transmitted from punched paper tape in Auto mode, this feat could not have been accomplished. When two identical ciphertext are added together, the sum characters are all / / / / ...../. Thus the errors of abbreviation and misspellings by the originating operator opened the door to breaking the cipher and determining the design of the Lorenz machine.

Determining the Design of the Lorenz Machine

The next problem was to uncover the design of a machine that could produce the approximately 4,000-character key recovered by Col. Tiltman. Col. Tiltman was sure that the Germans were using a machine and not two tapes as with the Vernam and Morehouse patents. This much was assumed, or known: the machine had pinwheels with two sets of five wheels and two wheels with some unknown function. This was a straightforward deduction. Baudot codes have five bits and based on the Morehouse patent the assumption could be made that there were two sets of five wheels with two left over.

After several months of work with no results, the task of finding the patterns in the key was given to Bill Tutte, a young chemistry graduate who had taken an introductory course in cryptology and had been assigned to GCHQ. Bill started by looking for cycles or repeats in the key. As described earlier, a determination had been made from ciphertext indicators that there were eleven indicator positions using 25 letters (J was omitted) and one used 23 letters. He guessed that the key could have a period of 23 or 25, or even 25×23 = 575. Although Bill didn't have much faith in this procedure, he wanted to look busy and gave it a try. [12]

Recall that the Baudot code has five channels (the five punches on the tape). Tutte selected channel #1 of the key (called the first impulse at GCHQ) and listed the "ones" and "zeros" in length 575 as shown in Figure 3.3. With approximately 4,000 characters, there were almost seven rows in this table. In other words, Tutte was overlapping short segments of the long key (channel 1) into shorter keys looking for depth that would indicate a cycle in the key.

---

* Note that spaces are not usually inserted between words, only between sentences.

† The dates are not clear from the record.

‡ We cannot reconstruct the complete process; we do not know the ciphertext messages as they have not survived.

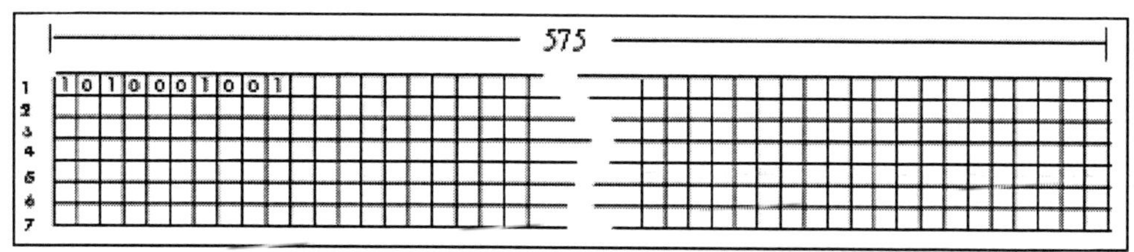

Figure 3.3 Tutte's First Attempt

There were only a few pattern repeats in the vertical direction that would indicate a period of 575. However, there were repeats on diagonals. Tutte then tried a period of 474 with the result that a number of repeat patterns of length 5 or 6 were found. Progress was being made.

The period of 574 did not have enough repeats so a period of 41 was tried. Forty-one is a factor of 574 and is a prime number, making it a likely candidate. The array of 41 columns and 98 rows yielded results with a large number of repeats in the columns. There were enough repeats in the key for Tutte to draw the conclusion that channel #1 had a period of 41. That is, the pinwheel for channel #1 had 41 pins. *

Further analysis of channel #1 revealed that there were two pinwheels forming the Key' sequence by mod2 addition: one wheel having 41 pins and the other having 43 pins. The number of pins is the cycle length of the wheel. These two wheels corresponded to one channel of the two tapes of the Morehouse system and were called the Chi and Psi wheels. Some authors have called these wheels *K* and *S*. However, in this book, the symbols *X* and *S* are used, which is consistent with contemporary authors' usage.

Tutte also discovered the *X* wheel moved in step with every enciphered letter while the *S* wheel moved in an irregular pattern. Sometimes the *S* wheel moved on each letter and at other times it did not move. With this discovery by Tutte, the whole Research Section turned to find the other wheel periods and to discover the cause of the irregular movement of the *S* wheels.

The irregular *S* wheel movement was found to be controlled by the remaining two wheels, called Motor Wheels. *M*1 had 61 pins and *M*2 had 37 Pins. *M*1 stepped on every letter; when *M*1 was a "one" *M*2 stepped. When *M*2 was a "one" the *S* wheels (all 5 of them) stepped. Hence thc serial stepping of the motor wheels controlled the irregular stepping pattern of the S wheels. The period of motor wheel stepping was $61 \times 37 = 2{,}257$ and the motor wheel cycle would have begun to repeat on the 4,000-character message.

The wheels and their cycles are repeated from Chapter 2.

*X*1	41	*S*1	43	*M*1	61
*X*2	31	*S*2	47	*M*2	37
*X*3	29	*S*3	51		
*X*4	26	*S*4	53		
*X*5	23	*S*5	59.		

One year after the first teleprinter signals were heard and six months after the August 30 message, GCHQ had determined the design of the Lorenz cipher machine. True, the wheel pin patterns and settings were known for only this one message but with

* What Tutte did was to stack the message in depth for the channel #1 pinwheel.

the skills at GCHQ, the path was open to read a large fraction of messages transmitted by this system.

There were several reasons that Tiltman and Tutte were able to make this breakthrough. First, two almost identical messages were transmitted with the same pinwheel patterns and wheel setting. This allowed the depth analysis made by Col. Tiltman that produced the Key' for the messages. Reusing a key is a cardinal sin of cryptography. Bill Tutte's idea of using two wheels was an application of key reuse. This and his dogged determination to find the pin patterns of the key yielded astounding results.

A major goof by the Germans in the creation of the wheel pin patterns provided the second break for Col. Tiltman. The *S* and *M* wheels were programmed so that there were relatively long stretches of characters between changes in the pattern of the *S* wheels. With these relatively long stretches the second key, *S*, was a constant and the *S* wheels did not completely obscure the period of the *X* wheels.

Once the period of the *X* wheels was found, the pin patterns could be found as well as the obscuring *S* wheel periods and pin patterns. The break-in to the design of the Lorenz machine had been accomplished.

When referring to the Germans sending two long messages in depth and their design of the *S* wheel patterns, Tutte observed the following: "Either error without the other the Germans would, I think, have gotten away with."[13]

A fourth reason was the procedure used by the Germans to encipher the message serial number in the ciphertext. This encipherment gave Col. Tiltman a strong crib into the plaintext. The placement of the messaged serial number changed during the war as discussed in Chapter 9.

Shortly after August 30, 1941, the Germans changed the programming of the *S* and Motor wheels, which presented a random pattern of changes in the *S* keys, discussed in Chapter 9. However, with the one message of August 30, enough had been learned by GCHQ of the design of the Lorenz machine that analogs could be built, named Tunny, after the name given to the first broken link machines and described in Chapter 10.

Source of Fish Interceptions

The British Y Service had the responsibility of operating the interception stations that received all German radio signals. Starting in mid 1941, various Y service stations intercepted Fish traffic. A dedicated station for Fish intercepts was established in mid-1942 on a 500 foot hill about 15 miles southeast of London near the villages of Knockholt and Biggin Hill, Figure 3.4. A staff of 600 intercepted messages from twelve Fish links.[14] [15]

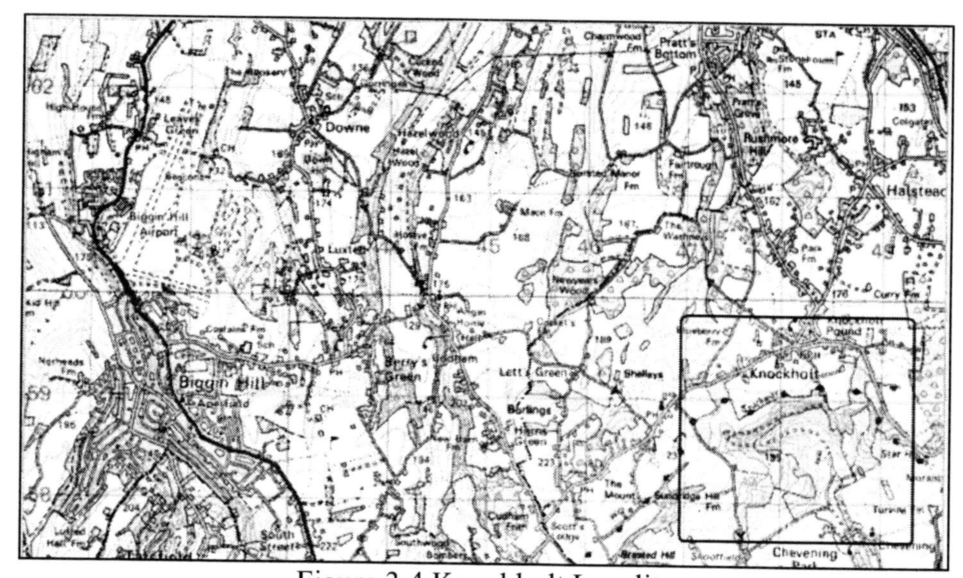

Figure 3.4 Knockholt Locality
(Reproduction by kind permission of Ordnance Survey © Crown Copyright NC/03/4786)

The intercepts were received and recorded on an undulator, a device similar to a strip chart recorder that recorded the serial transmission of the five bit Baudot code, Figure 3.5.[*] [16] The British Creed Teleprinters were not as fast as the German teleprinters, thus direct teleprinter reception was not possible.

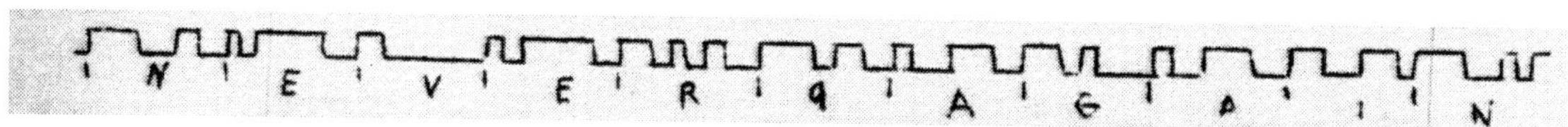

Figure 3.5 Undulator tape

Two trained operators could read an undulator tape and type out the Baudot equivalent creating two punched paper tapes. The two tapes were overlaid and accepted only if there were fewer than six errors. High priority intercepts were sent to GCHQ via two of six dedicated teleprinter landlines. [17] [†] Land line error checking was achieved by transmitting each tape over two landlines from separated readers, lines, and receiver teleprinter. Lower priority intercept tapes were sent to GCHQ by motorcycle courier.

Summary

After the August 30, 1941 message was broken and the design of Lorenz established, the operational link, Athens-Vienna, was broken by hand in early 1942. With this success, GCHQ concluded that decoding machines, which would be analogs of Lorenz, would be needed to mechanize the deciphering process. The first of these machines, called Tunny, were ordered. In December, 1942, Max Newman[‡] formed a new

---

[*] The name undulator is used today by physicists to identify a device that produces undulations in an electron beam.

[†] Instruction was given to Knockholt as to the characteristics of messages that were deemed priority. Examples are messages in depth with the same indicators and messages between Berlin and an active Army Headquarters.

[‡] A. Turing had been a student of Newman at Cambridge University.

organization to research and exploit machine methods for performing wheel setting and wheel breaking of Fish traffic.

This chapter has given a brief overview of the momentous events of 1940, 1941, and 1942. These events are summarized in Figure 3.6, a time line for these three years. The only word that can describe these events is *remarkable*. In a period of time of approximately one and one half years, from the time that the first teleprinter signals were received, current traffic was being read for the first time.

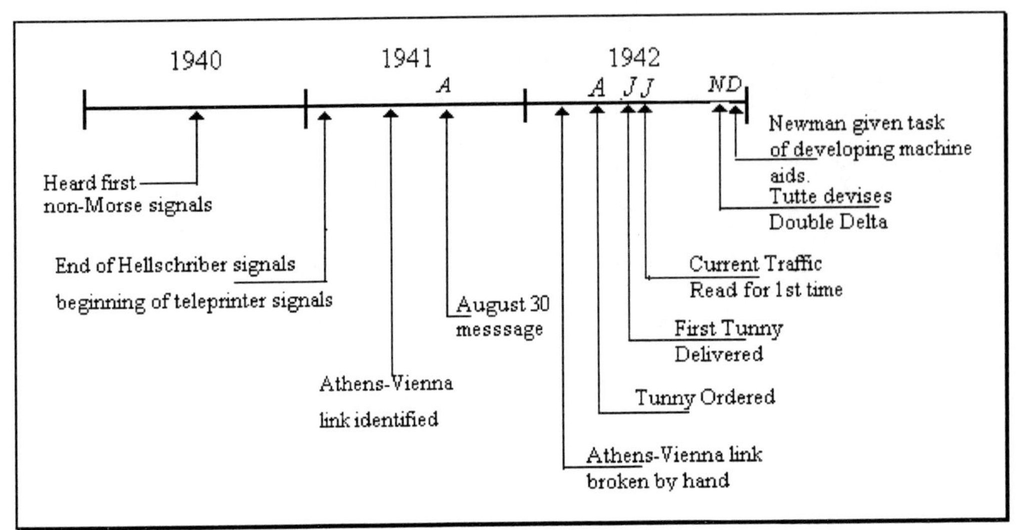

Figure 3.6 Early Time Line

References

[1]Michie, D., Good, J., Timms, G., *General Report on Tunny*, 1945, Released to the Public Record Office in 2000, http://www.alanturing.net/tunny_report, pg. 304.
[2] Email Tony Sale, July 2002.
[3] (Michie, *General Report on Tunny*, 297).
[4] (ibid, 297).
[5] (ibid, 298).
[6] Anonymous, *Principles of Solution of Cryptograms Produced by the IT&T Cipher Machine,* Technical Paper of the Signal Intelligence Section, War Plans and Training Division, USGPO, 1934, NARA, RG457, Box 745.
[7] Morgan, G. W., "Theory and Analysis of a Letter-Subtractor Machine". RG 457, Box 185, National Archives. Date unknown.
[8] Jacobs, W., *Cryptanalysis of Tunny Cipher Devices",* April 14, 1945, *NARA*, RG457, Box 943, Pg. 3.
[9] (Michie, *General Report on Tunny*, 364).
[10] www.mariner.org/atlantic/ photos/images/ttb02.jpg.
[11] Marks, L. *Between Silk and Cyanide*, Touchstone Book, New York, 1998.
[12] Tutte, W., "FISH and I" University of Waterloo, June 19, 1998. http://frode.home.cern.ch/frode/crypto/tutte.html, pg. 5.
[13] (ibid. 6).
[14] Smith, M., *Station X: Decoding Nazi Secrets*, TV Books, 1988, pg. 188-9.
[15] Anonymous, *Report on British Attack on "Fish"* Communications Intelligence Technical Paper TS 47, Navy Department, May 1945. NARA RG 457, Box 607, pp. 17-18
[16] (Anonymous, *Report on British Attack on "Fish",* 12).
[17] (Michie, *General Report on Tunny*, 281).

Chapter 4

Wheel Setting

Background

By the summer of 1942, Bletchley Park knew the design of the Lorenz cipher machine. They were also able to establish the wheel pin patterns for a ciphertext message by a process called Wheel Breaking. Wheel breaking was done by cryptographic analysis of messages in much the same way that the August 30, 1941 message was broken (discussed further in Chapter 5). What was not known was a robust method to find the wheel setting, the initial position of the twelve wheels, of the keytext used to encipher a plaintext message. Wheel setting is required to decipher the message.

If the wheel setting is known, the key can be subtracted from the ciphertext message, character by character, to give the plaintext message. If the subtraction is done without the correct wheel setting, the result of the subtraction will be gibberish.

Recall that each message should have had a unique wheel setting. Therefore, wheel setting for all of the intercepted messages became a first priority. Only if wheel setting could be found on a routine basis could the large volume of messages be broken. The job of wheel setting was the major task until July 1944 when the Germans instituted daily wheel pattern changes. After that date wheel breaking assumed a role of equal importance at GCHQ.

This chapter describes how a procedure was developed that computed wheel settings based on the statistics of a single ciphertext message. As a consequence of the use of statistics machine aids were required to process the high volume of data contained in a ciphertext message.

Two machine types were developed at GCHQ for wheel setting, Robinson (Chapter 7) and Colossus (Chapter 8). Colossus was applied to wheel breaking, using statistical processes, at a later critical time.

The Enciphering Equation

A Lorenz-machine enciphered message can be described by the equation:

$$\text{Ciphertext} = X \oplus S' \oplus \text{Plaintext}$$

$$Z = X \oplus S' \oplus P$$

and

$$Z \oplus X = S' \oplus P$$

The use of the term *S'* needs explanation. The *S* wheels step under the control of the *M* wheels. As the stepping is intermittent, with some enciphered characters the *S* wheels do not move. Thus the *S* pattern was "stretched", a pattern called *S'*. For example, if the *S* wheel pattern were PBAJ, the stretched pattern may be PPPBBAJJ. Thus the actual encipherment used *S'*, not *S*.

The enciphering equation above can be expressed in two equations with a new term "Pseudo Plaintext", discussed later in this chapter.

1. Pseudo Plaintext = Ciphertext ⊕ X

$$D = Z \oplus X$$

2. Pseudo Plaintext = Plaintext ⊕ S'.

$$D = S' \oplus P$$

The task facing GCHQ was to solve these two equations for each ciphertext message intercepted from the Germans. Solving the first equation, $D = Z \oplus X$, required heavy mathematical and statistical prowess and was the responsibility of the section headed by Max Newman, called the Newmanry. Essentially this section had to discover the pin patterns of the X wheels and the starting position of the X wheels when enciphering a message, a process called Wheel Setting. The end product of the Newmanry was the Pseudo Plaintext of a cipher message.

Solving equation 2 required a great deal of cryptographic and linguistic skills in order to extract S' wheel patterns and the plaintext from the pseudo plaintext. Solution of equation 2 was the task of a section called the Testery headed by Maj. Ralph Tester.* In addition, the Testery determined the wheel pin patterns and settings of the S and M wheels, tasks discussed in Chapter 6. The output of the Testery was the wheel patterns and settings for the S and M wheels. These along with the patterns and settings of the X wheels were used to find German Plaintext on the Tunny machine described in Chapter 10.

This chapter describes the work of the Newmanry in determining the X wheel settings and the pseudo plaintext for a single ciphertext message. Wheel setting is described before wheel breaking as some of the concepts are more apparent and the early effort at GCHQ was concentrated on this task.

The Statistical Approach to Wheel Setting

For a number of years, up until 1944, wheel breaking was performed by cryptographic means and wheel setting was the first task to be attacked mathematically. What was done to solve the problem of wheel setting? The available evidence indicates that Bill Tutte was the creator of a wheel setting system that was reasonably accurate and could be mechanized on primitive machines.[1]

Extensive tests were made on intercepted ciphertext messages (after August 30, 1941) and it was found that there was no statistical information in a single channel; the ratio of ones to zeros was 0.5. Nor was there statistical information in the *differences* between the nth and n+ 1 characters of a single channel. How the Germans achieved this characteristic is described in Chapter 9. The use of first differences† seems to have been well known at GCHQ at the time as described in Morgan's paper and his note on the use of differences. [2]

Each channel of plaintext and each channel of the keytext would produce channels of ciphertext as:

---

* Ralph Tester had extensive business experience in Germany prior to the war and was expert in the German language.

† Also, could be called the first derivative.

For a single channel:

$$Z_i = X_i \oplus S'_i \oplus P_i$$

Where i = the channel: 1,2,3,4,and 5

The symbol Δ signifies the difference. For example, the bits for the ith channel of the ciphertext Z is:

$\Delta Z_{i,n} = Z_{i,,n} \oplus Z_{i,(n+1)}$.
Where i = channel (1,2,3,4,5)
n = character number (1,2,...n).

That is: the Δ for the ith channel is the difference between the nth and n[th+1] characters of that channel. For a Δ value, the subscripts for the character number are implied and dropped from the notation.

The enciphering equation of a single channel in Δ form is:

$$\Delta Z_i = \Delta X_i \oplus \Delta S'_i \oplus \Delta P_i.$$

A large volume of statistical data on the Δ form of each of the five channels of the ciphertext Z was examined. This examination showed that there was no statistically valid information in one channel. The ratio of 1 to 0 was 0.5.

Tutte posited the idea: even though there was no statistical information in the delta of a single channel, there should be statistical information in the combination of two channels.*

The enciphering equation for channels 1 and 2 becomes:

$$(\Delta Z_1 \oplus \Delta Z_2) = (\Delta X_1 \oplus \Delta X_2) \oplus (\Delta S'_1 \oplus \Delta S'_2) \oplus (\Delta P_1 \oplus \Delta P_2).^{\dagger}$$

A second idea concerned the statistical properties of the Δ form of two channels of the S' wheels and the plaintext. Tutte had two hypotheses:

1. $(\Delta S'_1 \oplus \Delta S'_2) = 0$ (most of the time, on the assumption that the S wheels stepped infrequently).
2. $(\Delta P_1 \oplus \Delta P_2) = 0$ (most of the time, base on the analysis of German plaintext).

Stated another way:

1. $P[(\Delta S'_1 \oplus \Delta S'_2) = 0] > 0.5$
2. $P[(\Delta P_1 \oplus \Delta P_2) = 0] > 0.5$.

If these two hypotheses are correct, then most of the time

---

* This conjecture later proved mathematically to be correct. This proof is discussed further in Chapter 9 and Appendix D.

† The record is not clear as why Tutte selected channels 1 and 2 and not two others.

$(\Delta Z_1 \oplus \Delta Z_2) = (\Delta X_1 \oplus \Delta X_2)$
and
$P[(\Delta Z_1 \oplus \Delta Z_2) \oplus (\Delta X_1 \oplus \Delta X_2) = 0] > 0.5.$

In other words, when channels 1 and 2 of the keytext and the ciphertext characters are examined character by character, if they are in the same alignment as during the enciphering process, $(\Delta Z_1 \oplus \Delta Z_2) \oplus (\Delta X_1 \oplus \Delta X_2) = 0$ most of the time. If the keytext and ciphertext are not in alignment, then $(\Delta Z_1 \oplus \Delta Z_2) \oplus (\Delta X_1 \oplus \Delta X_2) = 1$ less than half of the time.*

The way the alignment is found is to perform the operation, $(\Delta Z_1 \oplus \Delta Z_2) \oplus (\Delta X_1 \oplus \Delta X_2)$ and count the times that the result is zero. This operation is performed for each pair of ciphertext and keytext deltas for each character in the cipher message. The wheel setting or alignment with the largest score of zeros is the most likely *X* wheel setting or starting position.

The hypothesis and method of finding the setting of the *X* wheels is now called The Double Delta Algorithm.† Tutte considered two channels and wheels; the problem is computationally tractable with mechanical aids and yielded valid statistical results for the most probable wheel setting.

First Hypothesis

Let us look now at the hypothesis that $P[(\Delta S'_1 \oplus \Delta S'_2) = 0] > 0.5$ (that is, most of the time). Tutte calculated that $P[(\Delta S'_1 \oplus \Delta S'_2) = 0] = 0.7$.[3] In other words, most of the time is really 70% of the time. How might he have arrived at this value? A contrived example is given that may be similar to the process used by Tutte.

Consider Table 4.1, showing the sixteen values of n and n+1 characters of *S'* wheels 1 and 2. In this table, $S'_{1,1}$ is wheel 1 and n = 1. $S'_{2,2}$ is wheel 2 and n =2. The mod2 sum of four values is 1 when the number of 1's are odd signifying that the *S'* wheels have changed.‡ When the number of 1's is even, the *S'* wheels have not changed.

In other words, the *S'* wheels have not changed when the two values in columns 1,2 are the same (0,0 or 1,1) and columns 3,4 are the same (0,0 or 1,1) of the table.§ There are four non-change states, as shown in the last column.

* The setting position given by the indicators was known but not the relationship between the indicators and the wheel pin patterns for that message.

† This algorithm was known at GCHQ by the Robinson/Colossus notation, described in Appendix E, as 1+2* or 1+2 Break-in.

‡ The word "change" is used instead of "move" because even when the *S* wheels move there may be no change in *S*'.

§ Remember that all *S* wheels either step or do not step, thus the And requirement.

Table 4.1 S' Wheel Change

Channel 1		Channel 2			
$S'_{1,1}$	$S'_{1,2}$	$S'_{2,1}$	$S'_{2,2}$	$S'_{1,1} + S'_{1,2} + S'_{2,1} + S'_{2,2} = (\Delta S'_1 + \Delta S'_2)$	S' wheels change?
0	0	0	0	0	no
0	0	0	1	1	
0	0	1	0	1	
0	0	1	1	0	no
0	1	0	0	1	
0	1	0	1	**0**	
0	1	1	0	**0**	
0	1	1	1	1	
1	0	0	0	1	
1	0	0	1	**0**	
1	0	1	0	**0**	
1	0	1	1	1	
1	1	0	0	0	no
1	1	0	1	1	
1	1	1	0	1	
1	1	1	1	0	no

For each of the four non-changes, the conjecture is correct, the value of $(\Delta S'_1 \oplus \Delta S'_2) = 0$. Further, it was estimated by GCHQ from the analysis of the motor wheels that the S wheels do not move 70% of the time (see chapter 9, a = 0.703). For these conditions, S' does not change. Thus these four states constituted 70% of the active states.

For the other 12 states, 4 of the states (indicated in **Bold**) have $(\Delta S'_1 \oplus \Delta S'_2) = 0$. Assuming that these states are equally probable, the weighted probability of $(\Delta S'_1 \oplus \Delta S'_2) = 0$ is:

$$P\,[(\Delta S'_1 \oplus \Delta S'_2) = 0] = 0.7 \times 1 + 0.3(4/12) = 0.7 + 0.1 = 0.8.$$

This probability roughly agrees with Tutte's value of 0.7.

Second Hypothesis

The question of the validity of the hypothesis that $(\Delta P_1 \oplus \Delta P_2) = 0$ (most of the time) will now be addressed. Tutte recognized the relative high frequency of repeated letters in German plaintext; for example SS and MM. Kullback give statistics that show that 3.3% of all German digraphs* are repeats.[4] Further, some of the high frequency sequential letter pairs, such as S ⊕ E = 0 for channels 1 and 2.

Tutte states that the analysis of German military messages shows that

$$P\,[(\Delta P_1 \oplus \Delta P_2) = 0] = 0.6 \text{ or a little more.}$$[5]

One source of published data on 3,200 characters of ΔP is shown in Table 4-2[6] ; other data can be found elsewhere.[7] From the ΔP data in the table we can compute the

* Pairs of consecutive letters.

number of times that two characters when added together give a particular ΔP character.* For example, R can be the result of a number of consecutive characters that are added together. For instance: M ⊕ P = R, and Z ⊕ Figures (UC) = R. Consulting Figure 3.1 will show that there are 32 pairs of characters that will give R.

Table 4.2 ΔP of 3,200 Characters

ΔP Character	Count	%	Code	ΔP Character	Count	%	Code
Figure (UC)	361	11.3	11011	D	79	2.5	10010
U	196	6.1	11100	X	76	2.4	10111
Letter (LC)	157	4.9	11111	R	76	2.4	01010
Null, /	156	4.8	00000	Space	75	2.4	00100
Carriage Ret.	150	4.7	00010	C	73	2.2	01110
J	139	4.3	11010	H	72	2.2	00101
F	134	4.1	10110	*X*	68	2.1	11110
O	133	4,1	00011	W	67	2.1	11001
M	104	3.2	00111	Q	66	2.1	11101
A	102	3.2	11000	L	66	2.1	01001
G	100	3.1	01011	Line Feed	63	1.9	01000
Y	94	2.9	10101	N	61	1.9	00111
S	93	2.9	10100	T	58	1.8	00001
P	88	2.7	01101	I	55	1.7	01100
Z	82	2.5	10001	V	51	1.6	01111
E	81	2.5	10000	B	24	0.75	10011

Note that the highest frequency ΔP character is Figure(UC) with a count of 361 or 11.3% of all pairs in the 3,200-character sample.

Remember that we want to know the probability of $(\Delta P_1 + \Delta P_2) = 0$. Thus the first and second channels are added mod2. For channels 1 and 2 of the ΔP characters with 11 or 00, $\Delta P = 0$. The percentages for the ΔPs with zero result are underlined in Table 4.2. Summing the number of zero ΔPs from Table 4.2 we find the probability of zero ΔP to be 1,965/3,200 = 0.614.† That is:

$$P[(\Delta P_1 \oplus \Delta P_2) = 0] = 0.614.$$

Double Delta Wheel Setting

Recall the enciphering equation considering channels 1 and 2:

$$(\Delta Z_1 \oplus \Delta Z_2) = (\Delta X_1 \oplus \Delta X_2) \oplus (\Delta S'_1 \oplus \Delta S'_2) \oplus (\Delta P_1 \oplus \Delta P_2),$$

$$(\Delta Z_1 \oplus \Delta Z_2) \oplus (\Delta X_1 \oplus \Delta X_2) = (\Delta S'_1 \oplus \Delta S'_2) \oplus (\Delta P_1 \oplus \Delta P_2).$$

For each wheel setting, what is

$$P[(\Delta Z_1 \oplus \Delta Z_2) \oplus (\Delta X_1 \oplus \Delta X_2) = 0] = P[(\Delta S'_1 \oplus \Delta S'_2) \oplus (\Delta P_1 \oplus \Delta P_2) = 0]?$$

---

* Accumulating ΔP data required that messages be deciphered. As more messages were deciphered, the statistical validity of ΔP data increased.

† ΔP is a function of the nature of the plaintext, pure German or list of numbers for example. The habits of the originating operator affect ΔP; each of the links and each operator had distinguishing characteristics.

There are two conditions for $P[(\Delta S'_1 \oplus \Delta S'_2) \oplus (\Delta P_1 \oplus \Delta P_2) = 0]$. These are:

1. $P[(\Delta S'_1 \oplus \Delta S'_2) = 0]$ and $P[(\Delta P_1 \oplus \Delta P_2) = 0]$
2. $P[(\Delta S'_1 \oplus \Delta S'_2) = 1]$ and $P[(\Delta P_1 \oplus \Delta P_2) = 1]$.

$$P[(\Delta S'_1 \oplus \Delta S'_2) \oplus (\Delta P_1 \oplus \Delta P_2) = 0] = P[(\Delta S'_1 \oplus \Delta S'_2) = 0] \times P[(\Delta P_1 \oplus \Delta P_2) = 0] + P[(\Delta S'_1 \oplus \Delta S'_2) = 1] \times P[(\Delta P_1 \oplus \Delta P_2) = 1].$$

Substituting Tutte's two hypotheses:

$P[(\Delta S'_1 \oplus \Delta S'_2) = 0] = 0.73.$

$P[(\Delta P_1 \oplus \Delta P_2) = 0] = 0.614.$

$$P[(\Delta S'_1 \oplus \Delta S'_2) \oplus (\Delta P_1 \oplus \Delta P_2) = 0] = 0.8 \times 0.614 + (1\text{-}0.8) \times (1\text{-}0.614) = 0.49 + 0.077 = 0.567.$$ [*]

and

$$P[(\Delta Z_1 \oplus \Delta Z_2) \oplus (\Delta X_1 \oplus \Delta X_2) = 0] = 0.567$$

In other words, with favorable conditions, about 57% of the time, $(\Delta Z_1 \oplus \Delta Z_2) = (\Delta X_1 \oplus \Delta X_2)$ for each plaintext character and ciphertext character with the enciphering wheel setting. A probability of 0.57 may seem to be a small difference between the random value of 0.5, but with enough data, from a long ciphertext message, a definitive wheel setting can be found.

The length of a ciphertext message was between 2,000 and 25,000 characters.[†] The GCHQ found that wheel setting on short messages (say 2,000 characters) was usually unsuccessful because of the small statistical sample.

By using only channel 1 and channel 2, the effective key length is $41 \times 31 = 1{,}271$ characters. Thus the key length for setting wheels 1 and 2 was shorter than the cipher message and stacking in depth could be exploited. Using channels 1 and 2 so that depth could be exploited is another of Tutte's contributions.

In order to find the point of most likely wheel setting, channels 1 and two of the first character of the key, obtained from wheel breaking, will be aligned with channels 1 and 2 of the first character of the ciphertext and the double delta computed for each letter of the keytext and the ciphertext. The result called a *token* is either a 1 or 0.

$$\text{Token}_i = \Delta X_1 \oplus \Delta X_2 \oplus \Delta Z_1 \oplus \Delta Z_2 = X_{1,1} \oplus X_{1,2} \oplus X_{2,1} \oplus X_{2,2} \oplus Z_{1,1} \oplus Z_{1,2} \oplus Z_{2,1} \oplus Z_{2,2}$$

---

[*] Tutte gives the value of 0.55

[†] Recall from Chapter 2 that the Germans attempted to impose a maximum message length of 10,000 characters. However, messages over 10,000 characters are received daily and a message of 67,000 characters was once received.

The keytext is streamed past the Ciphertext and the zero tokens are counted, as shown in Figure 4.1. As the keytext is shorter than the ciphertext, the process is repeated until the ciphertext is exhausted. A score for this wheel setting is output. The score is displayed or printed.*

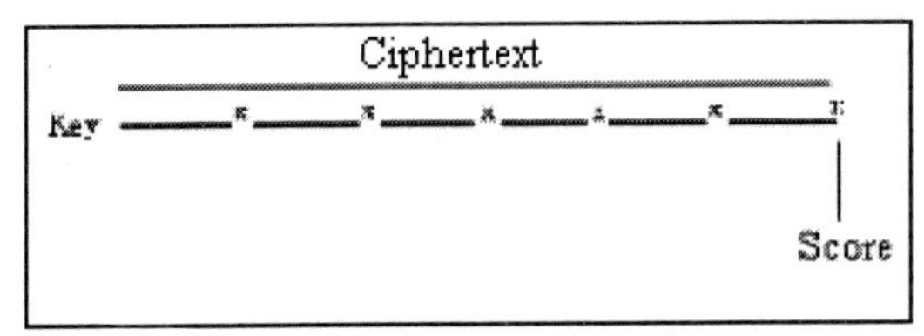

Figure 4.1 Computing Score

$$\text{Score of zero tokens} = (\text{token}_1 + \text{token}_2 + \ldots + \text{token}_n)$$ †

After one pass of the key against the ciphertext, the key is shifted one character and the process of Figure 4.1 is repeated as shown in Figure 4.2. The score is displayed or printed. This process continues until all 1,271 possible starting positions are scored.

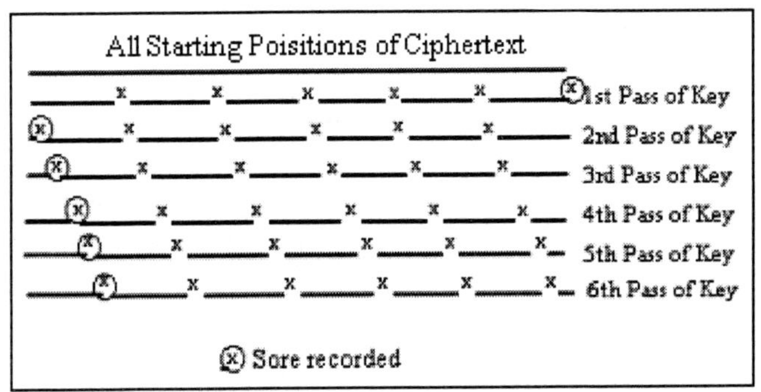

Figure 4.2 Additional Passes

The score of the double delta (the count of zero tokens) will be greatest when the ciphertext is aligned with the *X* wheel characters in the same setting used when the encipherment was performed. Greatest means the tokens are zero for approximately 0.55% of the total tokens. With the correct wheel setting for a 10,000 character ciphertext, 5,500 of the tokens should be zero. As stated previously, this is a very small statistical advantage over the expected random score of 5,000.

Each pass requires one double delta operation for each character of the ciphertext. The number of passes is the length of the key. Thus the number of double delta operations is:

Number of double delta operations = Length of $Z \times$ Length of X.

---

* Scores were displayed on lights with Robinson and recorded by operators. Scores on Colossi were printed on an Electromatic typewriter.

† It is tempting to compare this technique to William Friedman's Index of Coincidence. However, IC is derived for substitution ciphers, not additive ciphers. But Deavours and Kruh in Machine *Cryptography* imply that this was what was done at GCHQ; see page 20 for their discussion on Colossus.

Thus for a 10,000 character ciphertext and the 1,271 character key, over 12 million double delta operations are required to perform wheel setting. And, as each double delta operation requires seven Xor operations, 88.9 million Xor operations must be performed.

It should be obvious that this algorithm is not practical with only manual techniques. In Chapters 7 and 8 we will see how the streaming of ciphertext and keytext and performing the large number of operations and counts was accomplished on Robinson and Colossus.

Double Delta Example

The Tutte double delta algorithm is illustrated by a simple contrived example. The plaintext length for this example is much, much shorter than a typical actual message (30 vs. 10,000 characters). The plaintext *LUFTTEMPERATUR IN CELSIUS* [*] is crafted without word spaces but with a paragraph ending.[†] The key (M T F P R D repeated) is shown below the plaintext.

```
Plaintext: LUFTTEMPERATURINCELSIUS55M8899
Keytext:   MTFPRDMTFPRDMTFPRDMTFPRDMTFPRD
```

Figure 4.3 shows the plaintext with the Baudot characters, Channels 1 and 2 of the keytext and the ciphertext message as would be produced by the Lorenz machine under the assumption that the *S* wheels never moved, that is $\Delta S' = 0$ at all times.[‡]

With this simple message enciphered with a key, consider the method of finding the wheel setting using the double delta algorithm previously discussed. At GCHQ, the plaintext was obviously unknown and the key text had been found by cryptographic means prior to August 1944. What was not known was the wheel setting.

[*] Air temperature in Celsius.

[†] The characters 55M8899 are a standard ending, discussed in Chapter 6.

[‡] The method of correcting for this assumption is discussed in Chapter 6.

Plaintext		Plaintext-Baudot					Key		Cipher Text	
		1	2	3	4	5	1	2	1	2
1	L	0	1	0	0	1	0	0	0	1
2	U	1	1	1	0	0	0	0	1	1
3	F	1	0	1	1	0	1	0	0	0
4	T	0	0	0	0	1	0	1	0	1
5	T	0	0	0	0	1	0	1	0	1
6	E	1	0	0	1	0	1	0	0	0
7	M	0	0	1	1	1	0	0	0	0
8	P	0	1	1	0	1	0	0	0	1
9	E	1	0	0	0	0	1	0	0	0
10	R	0	1	0	1	0	0	1	0	0
11	A	1	1	0	0	0	0	1	1	0
12	T	0	0	0	0	1	1	0	1	0
13	U	1	1	1	0	0	0	0	1	1
14	R	0	1	0	1	0	0	0	0	1
15	I	1	1	1	1	0	1	0	0	1
16	N	0	1	1	0	0	0	1	0	0
17	C	0	1	1	1	0	0	1	0	0
18	E	1	0	0	0	0	1	0	0	0
19	L	0	1	0	0	1	0	0	0	1
20	S	1	0	1	0	0	0	0	1	0
21	I	0	1	1	0	0	1	0	1	1
22	U	1	1	1	0	0	0	1	1	0
23	S	1	0	0	0	0	0	1	1	1
24	5	1	1	0	1	1	1	0	0	1
25	5	1	1	0	1	1	0	0	1	1
26	M	0	0	1	1	1	0	0	0	0
27	8	1	1	1	1	1	1	0	0	1
28	8	1	1	1	1	1	0	1	1	0
29	9	0	0	1	0	0	0	1	0	1
30	9	0	0	1	0	0	1	0	1	0

Figure 4.3 Encipher Example

As discussed previously, the most likely wheel setting or alignment is found by testing all possible starting positions of the keytext. In this example the key text is 6 characters and 6 starting positions must be evaluated. The Token for each position is found by evaluating:

$$\text{Token}_i = \Delta X_1 \oplus \Delta X_2 \oplus \Delta Z_1 \oplus \Delta Z_2$$
$$= X_{1,1} \oplus X_{1,2} \oplus X_{2,1} \oplus X_{2,2} \oplus Z_{1,1} \oplus Z_{1,2} \oplus Z_{2,1} \oplus Z_{2,2}$$

for each character of the ciphertext and each of the six starting position of the keytext. *

The Score is the sum of the zero tokens and the maximum score is 30 in this example. However, using Tutte's value of 0.55, theory indicates an expected score of 30 × 0.55 = 16.5 with the correct wheel setting and the other settings will have an expected random score of 15.0.

Figure 4.4 shows the double delta procedure. The left-hand column shows the ciphertext as shown in the right-hand column of Figure 4.3. The second column shows the two characters of the keytext at the same wheel setting used for the encipherment in Figure 4.3. The double delta zero tokens and scores are computed with the scores shown

* Note that the token is the parity of the eight bits, $X_{1,1}$...... $Z_{2,2}$.

at the bottom of the columns. For zero shift (the enciphering setting), the score is 17, that is there are 17 zero tokens.

	Key Shifts					
Cipher Text	0 Tokens	1 Tokens	2 Tokens	3 Tokens	4 Tokens	5 Tokens
0 1	0 0 1	1 0 0	0 1 1	0 1 1	1 0 1	0 0 0
1 1	0 0 1	0 0 0	1 0 1	0 1 0	0 1 0	1 0 0
0 0	1 0 1	0 0 0	0 0 1	1 0 0	0 1 1	0 1 1
0 1	0 1 0	1 0 0	0 0 1	0 0 0	1 0 1	0 1 0
0 1	0 1 1	0 1 1	1 0 1	0 0 0	0 0 1	1 0 0
0 0	1 0 1	0 1 0	0 1 0	1 0 0	0 0 1	0 0 0
0 0	0 0 1	1 0 0	0 1 1	0 1 1	1 0 1	0 0 0
0 1	0 0 0	0 0 1	1 0 0	0 1 1	0 1 1	1 0 1
0 0	1 0 0	0 0 1	0 0 0	1 0 1	0 1 0	0 1 0
0 0	0 1 1	1 0 1	0 0 0	0 0 1	1 0 0	0 1 1
1 0	0 1 0	0 1 0	1 0 0	0 0 1	0 0 0	1 0 1
1 0	1 0 0	0 1 1	0 1 1	1 0 1	0 0 0	0 0 1
1 1	0 0 1	1 0 0	0 1 1	0 1 1	1 0 1	0 0 0
0 1	0 0 1	0 0 0	1 0 1	0 1 0	0 1 0	1 0 0
0 1	1 0 1	0 0 0	0 0 1	1 0 0	0 1 1	0 1 1
0 0	0 1 0	1 0 0	0 0 1	0 0 0	1 0 1	0 1 0
0 0	0 1 0	0 1 0	1 0 0	0 0 1	0 0 0	1 0 1
0 0	1 0 0	0 1 1	0 1 1	1 0 1	0 0 0	0 0 1
0 1	0 0 0	1 0 1	0 1 0	0 1 0	1 0 0	0 0 1
1 0	0 0 0	0 0 1	1 0 0	0 1 1	0 1 1	1 0 1
1 1	1 0 1	0 0 0	0 0 1	1 0 0	0 1 1	0 1 1
1 0	0 1 1	1 0 1	0 0 0	0 0 1	1 0 0	0 1 1
1 1	0 1 1	0 1 1	1 0 1	0 0 0	0 0 1	1 0 0
0 1	1 0 0	0 1 1	0 1 1	1 0 1	0 0 0	0 0 1
1 1	0 0 0	1 0 1	0 1 0	0 1 0	1 0 0	0 0 1
0 0	0 0 0	0 0 1	1 0 0	0 1 1	0 1 1	1 0 1
0 1	1 0 0	0 0 1	0 0 0	1 0 1	0 1 0	0 1 0
1 0	0 1 0	1 0 0	0 0 1	0 0 0	1 0 1	0 1 0
0 1	0 1 0	0 1 0	1 0 0	0 0 1	0 0 0	1 0 1
1 0	1 0 0	0 1 0	0 1 0	1 0 0	0 0 1	0 0 1
Score	17	16	14	14	14	13

Figure 4.4 Wheel Setting with Double Delta

The next column to the right shows the key shifted one position down (the bottom key character is shifted up to the top position) to give another alignment with a score of 16. Following to the right, the scores are 14, 14, 14, and 13.

Double delta theory posits that the setting with the greatest number of zeros is the most likely enciphering setting. For this example, the setting with the largest number of zeros (17) is the correct wheel setting. It may be surprising that this small example yields the correct result since the double delta algorithm is a statistical evaluation. The theory, developed earlier, indicates that the correct score will be $30 \times 0.55 = 16.5$, or either 16 or 17 for this example. Thus the score of 17 agrees closely with the theory.

The score of 16 is a possibility for the correct wheel setting. However this score, based on such a short ciphertext, is an example why short ciphertext messages would sometimes defy wheel setting by this method.

By this process, the correct wheel setting for channels 1 and 2 have been identified based only on the statistical analysis of the ciphertext stream and knowledge of the keytext. The wheel setting of the other wheels are found by a similar process. The massive number of calculations required for a real ciphertext message and keytext leads to the requirement for mechanical, or electronic, aids.

Finding Pseudo Plaintext, D and ΔD

The Newmanry needed to complete the work, noted earlier in this chapter, of finding the pseudo plaintext D and its ΔD of a ciphertext message. To follow this process we return to the basic equations for Lorenz encipherment.

$$Z = X \oplus S' \oplus P$$
$$\Delta Z = \Delta X \oplus \Delta S' \oplus \Delta P$$
$$\Delta Z \oplus \Delta X = \Delta S' \oplus \Delta P$$

A new term ΔD (Differenced Pseudo plaintext) is defined as:

$$\Delta D = \Delta Z \oplus \Delta X = \Delta S' \oplus \Delta P.$$

The ciphertext Z and ΔZ were known, as well as the keytext X and ΔX, and the correct wheel setting from the procedure described above. Thus mod2 addition (with the correct wheel setting) gives the pseudo plaintext D as well as ΔD. Pseudo plaintext is used in the Testery to discover $\Delta S'$ and S as well as the motor wheel patterns and settings, a process described in Chapter 6.

The ciphertext character stream could be in excess of 10,000 characters. Thus this operation on each of the characters of the key and ciphertext to form the plaintext and pseudo plaintext could not be done by hand reliably but required machine assistance. A Robinson or Colossus run produced the pseudo plaintext characters D punched on a paper tape, called a "de-chi tape."

Although nothing specific has been found in contemporary documents, there is an indication that both Robinson and Colossus were outfitted with paper tape punches, called perforators, which created the pseudo plaintext tapes. At the Testery, the de-chi tapes were printed out by a run on a special machine called Junior, which is described in Chapter 10.

Checking the Breaking and Setting of X Wheels

The process of finding the X wheel patterns* and wheel setting of a message involved a number of assumptions with slim statistical evidence. How can it be demonstrated that the resulting D and ΔD are probably correct solutions?

Various statistical tests were applied during the process of wheel breaking and wheel setting as checks on progress and ways to prevent following down dead-end paths. However one final test of the total process was used to compare the D and ΔD character stream output with known frequencies of occurrence of the various characters and bits within the characters. These known statistics were built up over many messages that had been successfully broken at GCHQ.

It was observed at GCHQ that the distribution of characters in a D stream is fairly random and would not help in determining if the character stream is D or just something else. However, a more reliable set of checks on the validity of the process uses the frequency of occurrence of ΔD as shown in Table 4.3.[8] These statistics are taken from

* At this point in the narrative, wheel breaking to find the wheel patterns is a manual process, described in Chapter 5. Later wheel breaking was assisted by Colossus runs, also described in Chapters 5 and 8.

messages deciphered at GCHQ. The Δ form of a character stream is always more sensitive to linguistic statistical variations.

Table 4.3 ΔD, 3,200 Characters

ΔD Character	Count	%	Code	ΔD Character	Count	%	Code
Figures (UC)	143	4.4	11011	Y	97	3.0	10101
Null, /	128	4.0	00000	I	96	3.0	01100
U	124	3.8	11100	A	96	3.0	11000
Carriage Ret.	113	3.5	00010	P	96	3.0	01101
Letters (LC)	112	3.5	11111	V	94	2.9	01111
Space	110	3.4	00100	R	92	2.8	01010
O	104	3.25	00011	L	92	2.8	01001
S	104	3.25	10100	Line Feed	90	2.8	01000
J	103	3.2	11010	C	90	2.8	01110
H	102	3.2	00101	*X*	89	2.8	11110
Q	101	3.2	11101	W	89	2.8	11001
F	100	3.1	10110	D	89	2.8	10010
G	100	3.1	01011	Z	89	2.8	10001
M	100	3.1	00111	E	89	2.8	10000
N	100	3.1	00111	X	87	2.7	10111
T	99	3.1	00001	B	82	2.6	10011

Two types of validity checks were used. One of the checks counted the frequency of occurrence of each of the ΔD characters. To perform this check on a Robinson, each character was counted in turn requiring 32 passes of the de-chi tape.* On each pass, the count of a character was made, recorded, and a manual comparison was made between the printed results and the accumulated database, such as Table 4.3. For example, if the correct wheel setting had been found, approximately 4% of all ΔD characters would be /. The random expected value for a monographically flat distribution is $1/32 \approx 3.1\%$, thus the difference between 4% and 3.1% is small but significant.

A second test is to count the occurrence of particular bit patterns in the de-chi tape. For example the pattern where both Channels 1 and 2 are ones (underlined in Table 4.3) can be counted. If the number of this pattern is approximately $857/3200 = 26.78\%$, the process is partially validated (a flat distribution would be 25%). The Newmanry had approximately 40 tests of this type.[9] Any significant deviation from the database would be cause to suspect that something, wheel breaking or wheel setting, was not correct.

The ΔD statistics varied from link to link. For example for the ΔD character /, three links have the following statistics: Tarpon, Bucharest to Berlin - 3.7%, Stickleback, Galatz to Berlin - 6.9%, and Bream, Rome to Berlin - 8.8%.[10] Therefore, the information collected at Knockholt on the origin (Rome, Berlin, etc.) of an intercept was critical to the checking process.

This test, when run on Colossus, helped to verify that correct D and ΔD tapes had been produced. Not until these tests had been made were the tapes classified "all certain" and sent to the Testery.[11]

* Robinson and Colossus possessed the flexibility to enable these character checks to be programmed by patching together the logic circuits to recognize a particular character. Colossus had five counters that reduced the number of passes to seven.

Statistical Test for Bulge

One of the tests performed after individual steps in the wheel setting process evaluated the statistical bulge, that is, compared the result with the random expected. This test was applied to see if a solution was valid or should not be trusted.

For example, the eight characters of ΔD, Table 4.3, with bits 1 and 2 both zero account for 128 + 110 + ... + 100 + 113 = 856 of the possible 3,200 characters. If the characters were random, 3,200 / 4 = 800 would have the first two bits equal to zero. This deviation from the random expected is called a bulge. There is a statistical bulge of 56 counts if the characters are actually from ΔD characters. The bulge can be expressed in a fraction: bulge = (856 – 800) / 3,200 = 0.0175.

Likewise, for a ΔD character stream of 3,200 characters the "11" bulge should be approximately 57 / 3,200 = 0.0178. Other tests were catalogued at GCHQ that looked not only at bits 1 and 2 but also bits 3, 4, and 5 in various combinations.[12]

Notation and Conclusion

Communications between the cryptanalysts and the operators of a Heath Robison or Colossus used an abbreviated format to specify the desired analysis. The notation is a language to specify what to count, the channels to be counted and any fixed conditions. Notation is discussed further in Appendix E.

A tribute to the Newmanry is found in Albert Small's report: "The job done by Newmanry today is miraculous, 95% of those marked all certain by Newmanry are broken on psi's [*S*] by Testery." [13]

References

[1] Michie, D., Good, J., Timms, G., *General Report on Tunny*, 1945, Released to the Public Record Office in 2000, http://www.alanturing.net/tunny_report/, pg. 288.

[2] Morgan, G. W., "Theory and Analysis of a Letter-Subtractor Machine". RG 457, Box 185, National Archives and Records Administration. Date unknown.

[3] Tutte, W., "FISH and I" University of Waterloo, June 19, 1998. http://frode.home.cern.ch/frode/crypto/tutte.html, pg. 7.

[4] Kullback, S., *Statistical Methods in Cryptanalysis*, Aegean Park Press, 1976, pg. 126.

[5] (Tutte, FISH, 7).

[6] Carter, F. L. "The Breaking of the Lorenz Cipher: An Introduction to the Theory Behind the Operational Role of "Colossus" at B.P. *IMA International Conference*, 1997.

[7] Anonymous, *Report on British Attack on "FISH"*, Communications Intelligence Technical Paper TS 47, Navy Department, Washington D.C., May 1945, RG 457, Box 607, pp. 20-21.

[8] Small, A. *Special Fish Report*, NARA, NR 4628 Box 1417, also http://www.codesandciphter.org.uk/documents/small/page112.html, December 1944.

[9] (ibid. 6).

[10] (Anonymous, *Report* ,22).

[11] (Small, *Special*, 5.

[12] (ibid, 5, 6).

[13] (ibid, 62).

Chapter 5

Wheel Breaking

Background

Wheel breaking was mandatory if the Fish messages were to be deciphered because the keytext was a necessary input to wheel setting, as discussed in Chapter 4. The Germans only changed the *X* pin patterns every month, until July 1944 when daily changes were instituted. Therefore, linguistic and cryptographic methods sufficed until July 1944. The following sections discuss the wheel breaking methods used at GCHQ by personnel in the Testery and the Newmanry. The methods described are: 1) cryptographic wheel breaking in the Testery and 2) statistical wheel breaking in the Newmanry and implementation on Colossus. After the wheel pin patterns were recovered, wheel setting proceeded as described in Chapter 4.

Testery Wheel Breaking Methods

The Testery was charged with the task of wheel breaking using linguistic and traditional cryptographic methods. The following descriptions of these methods are brief. One reason is that the few surviving descriptions were written to be read by people who were immersed in this work on a daily basis; therefore, they are incomplete. Another reason is that the techniques changed frequently as the security measures of the Germans changed. As a consequence, documentation of technique took second place to finding the next new technique. Available documentation of the work is consequently brief, incomplete and suffers from an inconsistent terminology.

Breaking by Depth

After the August 30, 1941 break-in, the design of the Lorenz machine was known, that is, the number of wheels, the number of pin positions for each wheel, and the purpose of each wheel (which wheel were *X*, *S* and *M*).

During the period of late 1942 to mid 1943, the Germans sent many messages in depth that were broken by GCHQ. Michie, Good and Timms wrote, "Fortunately the German operators began to send depths in great profusion, and so on many links it was still possible to read a fairly large fraction of the traffic."[1] Based on the prior experience, when these messages were intercepted, the wheel patterns were found with relative ease. The intercept station at Knockholt was on the alert for messages with the same indicators and these messages were given priority treatment.

However, a depth of two cannot always be broken because of the ambiguity between the two plaintext characters. The only way to resolve this ambiguity is to have a crib or some other evidence as to portions of the plaintext. It was the SPRUCHNUMMER crib that permitted Col. Tiltman to break the message of August 30, 1941.

For some time, the Germans use stylized salutations at the front of a message, giving an excellent cribbing opportunity. Over time, the Germans introduced padding words or sentences at the beginning of messages to defeat attacks by depth from cribs.

A registry of successful cribs was maintained at GCHQ that tied various links to cribs. This registry and the anticipated use of Proteus machines described in Chapter 10, provided assistance for cribbing.* Thus breaking by depth was an on-again, off-again endeavor.

Breaking by Near Depth

Recall that the message indicator was selected at random by the originating operator. Under heavy work loads, fatigue or sloth, sometimes two message indicators differed by only one character. These messages were said to have near depth. An example is taken from two messages received on April 22, 1942:[2]

```
1.  M H S L P E I S V O I U
2.  M H S L P E I . . O I U
```

There were statements in the plaintext preambles that these messages were the 3rd and 2nd parts of messages (presumably the same message). From experience, and crib information from the registry, the two messages were successfully found to begin with:

```
1.  DRITTER9TEIL9DES9SPRUNCHES9
2.   ZWOTER9TEIL9DES9SPRUNCHES9
```

Turing's Method

The break into the message of August 30, 1941was possible, in part, because the Germans had set the pins of the *S* and *M* wheels so that there were long stretches of characters between changes in the pattern of the *S* wheels. For these stretches, the enciphering equation was simply $Z = X \oplus P$.

After the Germans corrected their mistake in the pin patterns of the *S* and *M* wheels (the correction is discussed in Chapter 9), the method used by Col. Tiltman to break the August 30, 1941 message would no longer work. The ciphertext was corrupted by the *S* wheel movement. In addition, the introduction of QEPs (an indirect method of specifying indicators, discussed in Chapter 9) crippled the use of indicators for wheel breaking.[3]

What was needed was a method of wheel breaking from a single ciphertext message, that is, finding pin patterns of the *X* wheels from a single ciphertext message *Z*. Alan Turing studied the messages that had been broken and advanced an idea for attacking future messages.

Recall from Chapter 4 that the enciphering equation is:

$$\Delta Z_i = \Delta X_i \oplus \Delta S'_i \oplus \Delta P_i.$$

Turing defined the term, *K*, a composite key:

$$K = X \oplus S'^{\dagger}$$

* There is no evidence that a Proteus machine was ever completed.

† *K* is called KeyC in Chapter 2 and is not to be confused with the pseudo plaintext ΔD. This term is equivalent to the mod2 sum of the two Morehouse tapes.

and

$\Delta K = \Delta X \oplus \Delta S'$.

Reasoning that because the S wheels do not step most of the time (70% of the time, discussed in Chapter 9),

$P[\Delta S' = 0] = 0.70$.

Thus ΔK is the same as ΔX approximately 70% of the time.

The enciphering equation is reduced from

$Z = X \oplus S' \oplus P$

to

$Z = K \oplus P$

and

$\Delta P = \Delta Z \oplus \Delta K$

With a single ciphertext message, Z, the approach to finding P, and then S' and X, was to assume a starting value for ΔK, add it to the known ΔZ giving tentative pseudo plaintext ΔP. This pseudo plaintext would be highly garbled plaintext because the equality holds only about 70% of the time. However, with the linguistic skills in the Testery, the process yielded results and the true plaintext could be obtained from a single message.

When commenting on this approach, Tutte observes, "It is a method requiring great artistry. I never used it successfully myself. But there were others with whom it worked well enough."[4]

Newmanry Wheel Breaking from a Single Ciphertext Message

In 1942 Max Newman began to believe that mathematics needed to play a greater part in recovering the keys for the ever-increasing volume of Tunny traffic. Thus he established the Newmanry organization in December 1942 to assemble the personnel needed and to start working on the problem of mechanized wheel setting. Bill Tutte and other mathematicians were assigned to the Newmanry soon after. [5]

In July 1944, the Germans changed the procedures for the use of Fish. Each day, rather than each month, the wheel patterns were changed. The use of a unique wheel setting for each message was retained. This change in procedure ushered in a new period for GCHQ as wheel patterns had to be discovered every day for each of the dozen or so links. The necessity to find wheel patterns each day for each link lasted until the fall of Germany in May 1945. There is some evidence that the Newmanry started working on the theoretical problem of machine aided wheel breaking before December 1943.[6] And, Robinson wheel breaking may have been attempted in February 1944.[7] The GCHQ was prepared to cope with the problems of daily wheel pattern changes by the Germans.

Finding ΔX and X Wheel Patterns by Rectangling

What could be done to perform wheel breaking on the statistics of a single ciphertext message?

If probable values of ΔX_1 and ΔX_2 can be found, ΔX_1 and ΔX_2 can be integrated to find probable values of X_1 and X_2 .The process of integration is described later in this chapter. By this method, a probable keytext can be found from one cipher message that will feed into the wheel setting procedure described in Chapter 4

The first step was to find the most probable values of ΔX_1 and ΔX_2 by inference from $\Delta Z_1 \oplus \Delta Z_2$.

Recall from Chapter 4 that

$$P[(\Delta Z_1 \oplus \Delta Z_2) \oplus (\Delta X_1 \oplus \Delta X_2) = 0] = 0.57$$

The term $Z\oplus$ is defined as

$$Z\oplus = \Delta Z_1 \oplus \Delta Z_2$$

Thus $P[(Z\oplus) \oplus (\Delta X_1 \oplus \Delta X_2) = 0] = 0.57$

and

$$P[(Z\oplus = (\Delta X_1 \oplus \Delta X_2)] = 0.57$$

For a long ciphertext, many of the $Z\oplus$s are the result of enciphering with the same ΔX_1 and ΔX_2. Because the 1,271 values of ΔX_1 and ΔX_2 are reused several times, the $Z\oplus$s can be stacked in depth. For a 12,710 character ciphertext, there are ten reuses For example, the enciphered example of Figure 4.3 reuses the six character key five times, a depth of five.

Tutte, the acknowledged creator of this wheel breaking technique,[8] may have reasoned as follows. When dealing with only wheels X_1 and X_2, the key length is 1271 characters. As many cipher messages were 10,000 to 25,000 characters long, the $Z\oplus$s of the ciphertext messages can be written out as if there were a number of messages enciphered with the same key 1,271 character key. This procedure gives depth from one message (as far as $X1$ and $X2$ are concerned).* These messages will be called "simulated ciphertext messages."

An issue Tutte considered was finding a convenient graphical stacking format. A linear list of 1,271 characters was not attractive. His solution was to record the $Z\oplus$ values on a 41×31 rectangle (1,271 intersections) with the axis labeled ΔX_1 and ΔX_2.[9] Recording is from the upper left-hand corner downward to the right; at each intersection the value of $Z\oplus$ (1or 0) is recorded as shown in Figure 5.1. The 1,271 $Z\oplus$ values of simulated ciphertext message #1 will wrap around and fill up the rectangle. The next simulated ciphertext message is recorded and so on until all of the values are posted.

At this point, each intersection will have the $Z\oplus$ values that were enciphered with the same $X1$ and $X2$ key. In other words, the $Z\oplus$s are stacked in depth.

---

* This procedure is similar in concept to the Kasiski method for solving polyalphabetic ciphers.

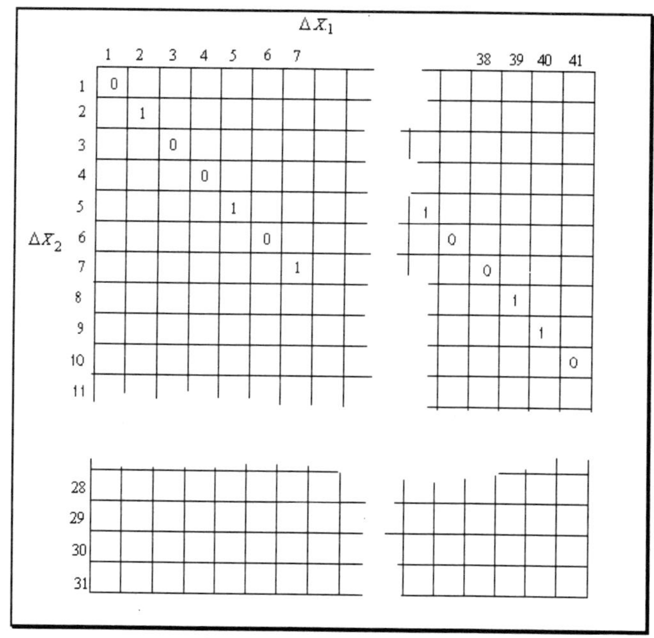

Figure 5.1 $Z\oplus$ Stacking

A second 41 × 31 rectangle was prepared and at each intersection, the surplus of 0s over 1s is posted as shown in Figure 5.2. For example, if there are six 1's and four 0's, the value posted is -2; the value will be positive if there is a surplus of 0's over 1's; the value will be 0 if the number of 0s and 1s are equal. These postings are called the "surplus-deficit."

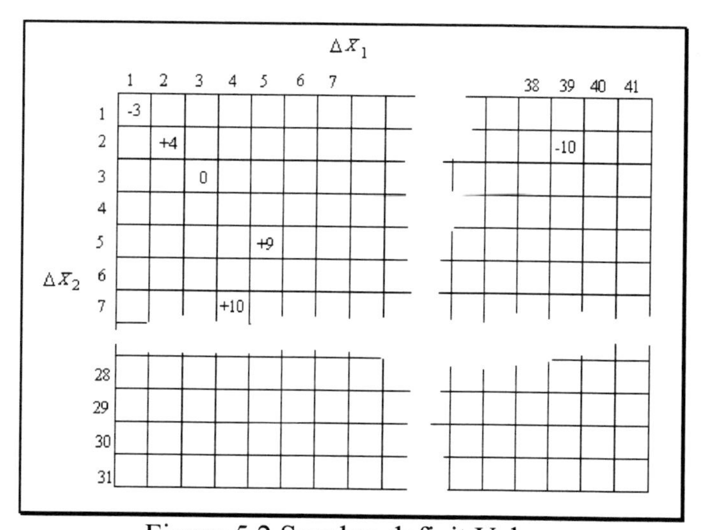

Figure 5.2 Surplus-deficit Values

Another rectangle was prepared, Figure 5.3, on which to post the most probable single bit values of $Z\oplus$. From the information of Figure 5.2 informed guesses were made as to the most likely values of $Z\oplus$. As shown in Figures 5.2 one intersection (2,39) had a surplus of 10 ones (-10) when the virtual stack is 10 deep. A strong case can be made for this intersection in Figure 5.3 that $Z\oplus = 0$.

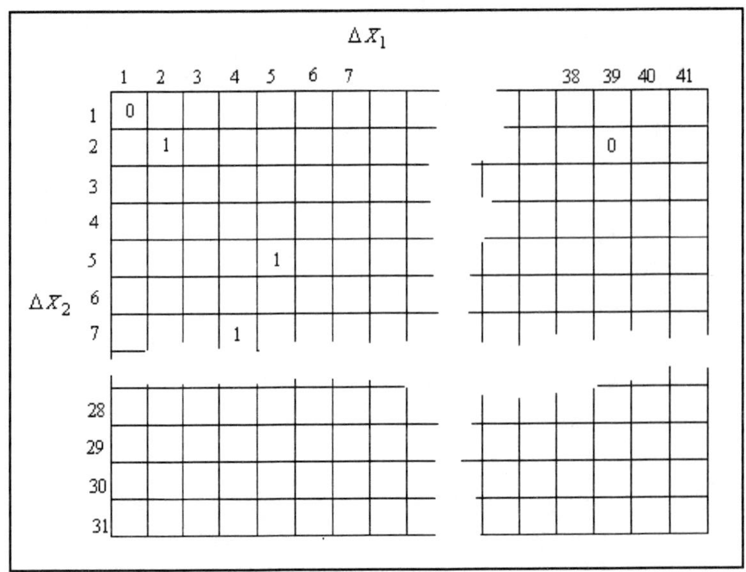

Figure 5.3 Most Probable Values of $Z\oplus$

When the most probable $Z\oplus$ estimates (one or zero) have been posted in the rectangle, the next step is to estimate the values of ΔX_1 and ΔX_2 that can best satisfy the values in the rectangle, $\Delta X_1 \oplus \Delta X_2 = Z\oplus$. One procedure to accomplish this goal is to set all the bits of ΔX_2 to 1 and see what values of $\Delta X1$ will satisfy the majority of the constraints imposed by the $Z\oplus$s in the rectangle.

From the best estimate of ΔX_2 find new values of ΔX_1 that will best satisfy the constraints of the $Z\oplus$s in the rectangle. This process is iterated back and forth until changes no longer occur; at this point the solution has converged to reasonable estimates for ΔX_1 and ΔX_2.* [10]

Rectangling Example

For an example of rectangling, consider $X1$ to be length 3 and $X2$ to be length 5. Thus the cycle of the key is 15. The pattern of $X1$ is (100) and $X2$ is (01100). A 67-character plaintext message *THEFURHERISTOT DERKAMFGEHTWEITER DOENITZ HEILHITLER* is given along with the first two channels of the key and ciphertext in Fig. 5.4.† The example does not consider the influence of the *S* wheels.

Only 65 characters of this 67-character message are used with this example. And, as the plaintext and ciphertext messages have 60 characters and the key is length 15, there will be four simulated ciphertext messages to stack. Note that the sequence 55M889 has been inserted between some words. This sequence is a common format for inserting full stops in text as discussed in Chapter 6.

* This process is roughly the inverse of Synthetic Annealing. The boundary conditions are found that will generate the array condition.

† The Furher is dead. The war goes on. Doenitz. Heil Hitler

	Plain Text, (P)					#	Key (X)								Ciphertext (Z)					Delta Ciphertext		
	1	2	3	4	5		1	2	3	4	5	$\Delta X1$	$\Delta X2$	$X\oplus$	1	2	3	4	5	$\Delta Z1$	$\Delta Z2$	$Z\oplus$
D	1	0	0	1	0	1	1	0				1	1	0	0	0				1	1	0
E	1	0	0	0	0	2	0	1				0	0	0	1	1				1	1	0
R	0	1	0	1	0	3	0	1				1	1	0	0	0				0	0	0
F	1	0	1	1	0	4	1	0				1	0	1	0	0				1	1	0
U	1	1	1	0	0	5	0	0				0	0	0	1	1				0	1	1
E	1	0	0	0	0	6	0	0				1	1	0	1	0				0	1	1
H	0	0	1	0	1	7	1	1				1	0	1	1	1				0	0	0
E	1	0	0	0	0	8	0	1				0	1	1	1	1				1	0	1
R	0	1	0	1	0	9	0	0				1	0	1	0	1				1	0	1
I	0	1	1	0	0	10	1	0				1	0	1	1	1				0	1	1
S	1	0	1	0	0	11	0	0				0	1	1	1	0				1	1	0
T	0	0	0	0	1	12	0	1				1	0	1	0	1				1	0	1
O	0	0	0	1	1	13	1	1				1	1	0	1	1				1	1	0
T	0	0	0	0	1	14	0	0				0	0	0	0	0				1	1	0
5	1	1	0	1	1	15	0	0				1	0	1	1	1				1	0	1
5	1	1	0	1	1	16	1	0				1	1	0	0	1				0	0	0
M	0	0	1	1	1	17	0	1				0	0	0	0	1				1	1	0
8	1	1	1	1	1	18	0	1				1	1	0	1	0				1	1	0
8	1	1	1	1	1	19	1	0				1	0	1	0	1				0	1	1
9	0	0	1	0	0	20	0	0				0	0	0	0	0				1	0	1
D	1	0	0	1	0	21	0	0				1	1	0	1	0				1	1	0
E	1	0	0	0	0	22	1	1				1	0	1	0	1				0	1	1
R	0	1	0	1	0	23	0	1				0	1	1	0	0				1	1	0
K	1	1	1	1	0	24	0	0				1	0	1	1	1				1	0	1
A	1	1	0	0	0	25	1	0				1	0	1	0	1				0	1	1
M	0	0	1	1	1	26	0	0				0	1	1	0	0				0	0	0
P	0	1	1	0	1	27	0	1				1	0	1	0	0				0	1	1
F	1	0	1	1	0	28	1	1				1	1	0	0	1				0	0	0
G	0	1	0	1	1	29	0	0				0	0	0	0	1				1	1	0
E	1	0	0	0	0	30	0	0				1	0	1	1	0				0	0	0
H	0	0	1	0	1	31	1	0				1	1	0	1	0				1	1	0
T	0	0	0	0	1	32	0	1				0	0	0	0	1				1	1	0
W	1	1	0	0	1	33	0	1				1	1	0	1	0				1	0	1
E	1	0	0	0	0	34	1	0				1	0	1	0	0				0	1	1
I	0	1	1	0	0	35	0	0				0	0	0	0	1				0	1	1
T	0	0	0	0	1	36	0	0				1	1	0	0	0				0	0	0
E	1	1	1	0	0	37	1	1				1	0	1	0	0				0	0	0
R	0	1	0	1	0	38	0	1				0	1	1	0	0				1	1	0
5	1	1	0	1	1	39	0	0				1	0	1	1	1				1	0	1
5	1	1	0	1	1	40	1	0				1	0	1	0	1				0	1	1
M	0	0	1	1	1	41	0	0				0	1	1	0	0				1	0	1
8	1	1	1	1	1	42	0	1				1	0	1	1	0				1	0	1
8	1	1	1	1	1	43	1	1				1	1	0	0	0				0	0	0
9	0	0	1	0	0	44	0	0				0	0	0	0	0				1	0	1
D	1	0	0	1	0	45	0	0				1	0	1	1	0				0	0	0
O	0	0	0	1	1	46	1	0				1	1	0	1	0				0	1	1
E	1	0	0	0	0	47	0	1				0	0	0	1	1				1	0	1
N	0	0	1	1	0	48	0	1				1	1	0	0	1				1	0	1
I	0	1	1	0	0	49	1	0				1	0	1	1	1				1	1	0
T	0	0	0	0	1	50	0	0				0	0	0	0	0				1	0	1
Z	1	0	0	0	1	51	0	0				1	1	0	1	0				1	0	1
5	1	1	0	1	1	52	1	1				1	0	1	0	0				1	0	1
5	1	1	0	1	1	53	0	1				0	1	1	1	0				1	0	1
M	0	0	1	1	1	54	0	0				1	0	1	0	0				0	1	1
8	1	1	1	1	1	55	1	0				1	0	1	0	1				1	0	1
8	1	1	1	1	1	56	0	0				0	1	1	1	1				1	0	1
9	0	0	1	0	0	57	0	1				1	0	1	0	1				1	0	1
H	0	0	1	0	1	58	1	1				1	1	0	1	1				0	1	1
E	1	0	0	0	0	59	0	0				0	0	0	1	0				1	1	0
I	0	1	1	0	0	60	0	0				1	0	1	0	1				1	0	1
L	0	1	0	0	1	61	1	0				1	1	0	1	1				1	0	1
H	0	0	1	0	1	62	0	1				0	0	0	0	1				0	1	1
I	0	1	1	0	0	63	0	1				1	1	0	0	0				1	0	1
T	0	0	0	0	1	64	1	0				1	0	1	1	0				1	1	0
L	0	1	0	0	1	65	0	0				0	0	0	0	1				1	1	0
E	1	0	0	0	0	66	0	0				1	1	0	1	0				1	0	1
R	0	1	0	1	0		1	1														

Figure 5.4 Sample Message

We now stack the values of $Z\oplus = (\Delta X_1 \oplus \Delta X_2)$ of the first fifteen simulated ciphertext messages into a 5 × 3 rectangle. The new entries for each step are in BOLD font. The first five bits of the first simulated ciphertext message are 00001posted in Step 1. The second five bits are 10111 posted in Step 2 and so on.

Step 1

	$\Delta X_{2,1}$	$\Delta X_{2,2}$	$\Delta X_{2,3}$	$\Delta X_{2,4}$	$\Delta X_{2,5}$
$\Delta X_{1,1}$	**0**			**0**	
$\Delta X_{1,2}$		**0**			**1**
$\Delta X_{1,3}$			**0**		

Step 2

	$\Delta X_{2,1}$	$\Delta X_{2,2}$	$\Delta X_{2,3}$	$\Delta X_{2,4}$	$\Delta X_{2,5}$
$\Delta X_{1,1}$	0	**0**		0	**1**
$\Delta X_{1,2}$		0	**1**		1
$\Delta X_{1,3}$	**1**		0	**1**	

Step 3

	$\Delta X_{2,1}$	$\Delta X_{2,2}$	$\Delta X_{2,3}$	$\Delta X_{2,4}$	$\Delta X_{2,5}$
$\Delta X_{1,1}$	0	0	**0**	0	1
$\Delta X_{1,2}$	**0**	0	1	**0**	0
$\Delta X_{1,3}$	1	**1**	0	1	**1**

Step 4

	$\Delta X_{2,1}$	$\Delta X_{2,2}$	$\Delta X_{2,3}$	$\Delta X_{2,4}$	$\Delta X_{2,5}$
$\Delta X_{1,1}$	**00**	0	0	**01**	1
$\Delta X_{1,2}$	0	**00**	1	0	**01**
$\Delta X_{1,3}$	1	1	**00**	1	1

Step 5

	$\Delta X_{2,1}$	$\Delta X_{2,2}$	$\Delta X_{2,3}$	$\Delta X_{2,4}$	$\Delta X_{2,5}$
$\Delta X_{1,1}$	00	**01**	0	01	**11**
$\Delta X_{1,2}$	0	00	**10**	0	01
$\Delta X_{1,3}$	**10**	1	00	**11**	1

Step 6

	$\Delta X_{2,1}$	$\Delta X_{2,2}$	$\Delta X_{2,3}$	$\Delta X_{2,4}$	$\Delta X_{2,5}$
$\Delta X_{1,1}$	00	01	**00**	01	11
$\Delta X_{1,2}$	**00**	00	10	**00**	01
$\Delta X_{1,3}$	10	**11**	00	11	**10**

This process continues until all 60 $Z\oplus$s of the 4 simulated ciphertext messages have been posted to the rectangle.

Final Posting

	$\Delta X_{2,1}$	$\Delta X_{2,2}$	$\Delta X_{2,3}$	$\Delta X_{2,4}$	$\Delta X_{2,5}$
$\Delta X_{1,1}$	0001	0101	0001	0110	1111
$\Delta X_{1,2}$	0011	0001	1001	0010	1111
$\Delta X_{1,3}$	1001	1111	0011	1111	1001

The next step creates another rectangle, similar to Figure 5.2, that records the surplus of 0's over 1's. Recall that Surplus = Number 0's - Number 1's. Zero indicates an equal number.

Surplus-deficit

	$\Delta X_{2,1}$	$\Delta X_{2,2}$	$\Delta X_{2,3}$	$\Delta X_{2,4}$	$\Delta X_{2,5}$
$\Delta X_{1,1}$	+2	0	+2	0	-4
$\Delta X_{1,2}$	0	+2	0	+2	-4
$\Delta X_{1,3}$	0	-4	0	-4	.0

Another rectangle, similar to Figure 5.3, is posted with the $Z\oplus$ one/zero evidence from the surplus-deficit rectangle. Where the surplus-deficit value is -4, there is strong

	ΔX_2				
ΔX_1	0		0	.	1
		0		0	1
		1		1	

evidence that Z⊕ = 1 for a given pair of ΔX_1 and ΔX_2.values. Likewise for +4, the evidence is that $Z\oplus$ = 0. The surplus-deficit of –2 and +2 are posted as 1 and 0 even though the evidence is not as strong. For the intersections with a surplus-deficit weight of 0, we have only a 50/50 chance of an assumed value (1 or 0) being correct and are shown shaded.*

Because this is a small contrived, example, ones and zeros are placed randomly to the intersections where the evidence is 50/50. By this step the rectangle is full and we can find a solution that illustrates the procedure.

	ΔX_2				
ΔX_1	0	1	0	1	1
	1	0	1	0	1
	0	1	0	1	1

A procedure for finding ΔX_1 and ΔX_2 is to assume a value for ΔX_1 and deduce the five bits of ΔX_2 based on the 1s and 0s in the rectangle. Then, using the five bits of ΔX_2 we work back and find three new bits of ΔX_1. The sweeps iterates back and forth until the solution converges.

For the first sweep, we choose ΔX_1= (111). Look first at $\Delta X_{1,1}$ =1; the values of ΔX_2 needed to match the first row of the rectangle are: (10100). Likewise for $\Delta X_{1,2}$ = 1, the values of ΔX_2 are (01010) and for $\Delta X_{1,3}$ =1, the values of ΔX_2 are (10100).

First Sweep, Find ΔX_2

		$\Delta X_{2,1}$	$\Delta X_{2,2}$	$\Delta X_{2,3}$	$\Delta X_{2,4}$	$\Delta X_{2,5}$
		1	0	1	0	0
		0	1	0	1	0
		1	0	1	0	0
$\Delta X_{1,1}$	**1**	0	1	0	1	1
$\Delta X_{1,2}$	**1**	1	0	1	0	1
$\Delta X_{1,3}$	**1**	0	1	0	1	1

* With a longer message, the number of cells in the rectangle with 0 should be small.

From the evidence just developed a majority vote for each bit gives ΔX_2 =(10100). We now take this estimate of ΔX_2 and make a sweep to estimate the bit values for ΔX_1.

Second Sweep, Find ΔX_1

		$\Delta X_{2,1}$	$\Delta X_{2,2}$	$\Delta X_{2,3}$	$\Delta X_{2,4}$	$\Delta X_{2,5}$
		1	**0**	**1**	**0**	**0**
$\Delta X_{1,1}$	1 1 1 1 1	0	1	0	1	1
$\Delta X_{1,2}$	0 0 0 0 1	1	0	1	0	1
$\Delta X_{1,3}$	1 1 1 1 1	0	1	0	1	1

This sweep indicates, by majority vote, that ΔX_1 is most likely (101). We now make the third sweep with ΔX_1 fixed at (101).

Third Sweep, Find ΔX_2

		$\Delta X_{2,1}$	$\Delta X_{2,2}$	$\Delta X_{2,3}$	$\Delta X_{2,4}$	$\Delta X_{2,5}$
		1	0	1	0	0
		1	0	1	0	1
		1	0	1	0	0
$\Delta X_{1,1}$	**1**	0	1	0	1	1
$\Delta X_{1,2}$	**0**	1	0	1	0	1
$\Delta X_{1,3}$	**1**	0	1	0	1	1

This sweep indicates that ΔX_2 is most likely (10100). We make a fourth sweep with this value of ΔX_2

Fourth Sweep, Find ΔX_1

		$\Delta X_{2,1}$	$\Delta X_{2,2}$	$\Delta X_{2,3}$	$\Delta X_{2,4}$	$\Delta X_{2,5}$
		1	**0**	**1**	**0**	**0**
$\Delta X_{1,1}$	1 1 1 1 1	0	1	0	1	1
$\Delta X_{1,2}$	0 0 0 0 1	1	0	1	0	1
$\Delta X_{1,3}$	1 1 1 1 1	0	1	0	1	1

The most likely value of ΔX_1 is (101), a value that has not changed from the Second Sweep. It seems that the process has converged. The results are summarized at this point and compared to the actual data from Figure 5.4.

	ΔX_1	ΔX_2
Rectangling	101	10100
Actual, Fig. 5.4	101	10101

In this example the values of ΔX_1 and ΔX_2 have been found from only the input of Z⊕s with only one bit in error. Remarkably, with the slim statistical evidence available in a single message a solution could be achieved. This method of wheel breaking works only if the ciphertext message is long enough. In such cases, the statistical odds favor a correct solution.

The reports on GCHQ's success with this technique state that messages of 25,000 characters (stacking of 20 simulated ciphertext messages) yielded satisfactory results.* Even with these long messages, extensive statistical tests were applied to estimate the degree of accuracy found with the determination of the values of the ΔX_1 and ΔX_2 wheels.

The amount of handwork required to rectangle a 20,000-character ciphertext can only be imagined. For this reason the mechanical aid of a Colossus was required if this procedure was to be useful. Fortunately, Donald Michie devised a method of setting up a Colossus to perform the first steps of rectangling. [11] This idea lead to an attachment to Colossus, described in Chapter 8, which mechanized this process when it was sorely needed, after July 1944, when the wheel patterns were changed every day.

Determining X from ΔX

A technique for determining *X from* ΔX is to integrate ΔX.[12] In addition to determining the *X*s, successful integration is a good test to see if the rectangling results are valid. Only if the integrated results were accepted were the results plausible. Remember that the statistical evidence is weak for the values of *X* found by this means. The technique will be illustrated by the values of ΔX_1 *and* ΔX_2 found in the example above and shown in Figure 5.4.

The process of integration can be described by examining the process of differencing one wheel pattern, which is a form of differentiation. For wheel X_1, and the characters 1 to n, differencing and integration are:

Differencing	Integration
$\Delta X_{1,1} = X_{1,1} \oplus X_{1,2}$	$X_{1,1} =$ One or Zero
$\Delta X_{1,2} = X_{1,2} \oplus X_{1,3}$	$X_{1,2} = \Delta X_{1,1} \oplus X_{1,1}$
$\Delta X_{1,3} = X_{1,3} \oplus X_{1,4}$	$X_{1,3} = \Delta X_{1,2} \oplus X_{1,2}$
*	*
*	*
$\Delta X_{1,n} = X_{1,n} \oplus X_{1,n+1}$	$X_{1,n} = \Delta X_{1,n-1} \oplus X_{1,n-1}$

We integrate ΔX_1 using the estimate for ΔX_1 = (101) found earlier. These three bits are recorded in Column #2 of the chart below. The bit $X_{1,1}$ can be either a 1 or 0; we start with 1. Integration is performed by solving the equations in sequence and extending a result in the right column into the left column: shown with the arrow. The result, (100) is in Column #1.

---

* Although messages over 10,000 characters were forbidden, originating operators would combine several short messages into one long message effectively giving one long message enciphered with one wheel setting. The receiving code clerk would break the messages apart using the enciphered message serial numbers.

Step	1	2	3
1		$X_{1,1}$	= 1
2	$X_{1,1}$	$\oplus \Delta X_{1,1}$	= $X_{1,2}$
	1	1	0
3	$X_{1,2}$	$\oplus \Delta X_{1,2}$	= $X_{1,3}$
	0	0	0
4	$X_{1,3}$	$\oplus \Delta X_{1,2}$	$X_{1,1}$
	0	1	= 1

Integrating ΔX_1 using this procedure we find that $X_1 = (100)$, as can be verified in Figure 5.4. This solution can also be verified by taking its Δ which gives (101). Because ΔX_1 has only three bits, the differencing process loops around to the first bit. Four steps are required to see if integration closes with the same value for $X_{1,1}$. This process will also converge if the initial assumption for $X_{1,1}$ was zero.

If we had started with 0 rather than 1, we would obtain the complement of the above solution, i.e. $X_1 = (011)$. There were statistical tests used to determine if the solution was correct. However, consulting Figure 5.4 will show that the (100) solution is correct.

Consider now the determination of X_2 from $\Delta X_2 = (10100)$ which is placed in Column #2 of the chart below. We start with Bit 1 of $X_2 = 0$. Following the integration procedure described above, we find that $X_2 = (01100)$ in Column #1 and as seen in Figure 5.4.

Step	1	2	3
1		$X_{2,1}$	= 0
2	$X_{2,1}$	$\oplus \Delta X_{2,1}$	= $X_{2,2}$
	0	1	1
3	$X_{2,2}$	$\oplus \Delta X_{2,2}$	= $X_{2,3}$
	1	0	1
4	$X_{2,3}$	$\oplus \Delta X_{2,3}$	$X_{2,4}$
	1	1	= 0
5	$X_{2,4}$	$\oplus \Delta X_{2,4}$	$X_{2,5}$
	0	0	= 0
6	$X_{2,5}$	$\oplus \Delta X_{2,5}$	$X_{2,1}$
	0	0	= 0

From the analysis above, we have decided that the likely value X_2 is $X_2 = (01100)$ which can be verified in Figure 5.4.* Because the S wheels were assumed to have no influence on the encipherment, this example is not totally realistic. The influence of the S

* It is interesting that the correct solution to X_2 was found even with ΔX_2 having one bit in error.

wheels increases the "noise" in the process but with sufficient depth, valid solutions were obtained.

Breaking the Other Wheels

After the values of ΔX_1 and ΔX_2 were found, the process was repeated for the other wheels. For example, ΔX_3 and ΔX_4 have a cycle $29 \times 26 = 841$. In this case, the rectangle will have 841 cells.

The bit values of ΔX_5 could be discovered in conjunction with one of the other wheel patterns that had been previously determined.

Conclusions

This chapter described how GCHQ was able to learn the *X* wheel patterns by two methods, cryptographic and statistical, from one ciphertext message. The latter approach, while theoretically interesting, was of little value if applied by manual means. The statistical approach demanded machine assistance, which was available with the introduction of Colossus.

Production processing of Fish ciphertext messages was then possible with machine aided wheel breaking and wheel setting. These machine aids, Robinson and Colossus are described in Chapters 7 and 8.

References

[1] Michie, D., Good, J., Timms, G., *General Report on Tunny*, 1945, Released to the Public Record Office in 2000, http://www.alanturing.net/tunny_report/, pg. 320.
[2] (ibid. 307).
[3] (ibid. 313).
[4] Tutte, W., "FISH and I" University of Waterloo, June 19, 1998. http://frode.home.cern.ch/frode/crypto/tutte.html, pg. 6.
[5] Smith, M., *Station X: Decoding Nazi Secrets*, TV Books, 1998, pg. 191.
[6] (Michie, *General Report,* 288).
[7] (ibid. 319).
[8] (ibid. 328).
[9] Anonymous, *Report on British Attack on "FISH",* Communications Intelligence Technical Paper TS 47, Navy Department, Washington D.C., May 1945, RG 457, Box 607, pg.62.
[10] (ibid. 62).
[11] Good, J., "Enigma and Fish". *Codebreakers, The Inside Story of Bletchley Park,* Ed. Hinsley, F. H., Stripp, A., Oxford University Press, 1993, pg. 164.
[12](Anonymous, *Report*, 74, 79).

Chapter 6

S Wheels, *M* Wheels and Plaintext

Background

The Newmanry produced the pseudo plaintext D by the methods described in Chapter 4. Recall that in these chapters, the influence of S' on the enciphering process was ignored. In other words, the assumption was made that the S wheels did not move and that $\Delta S = 0$. This assumption introduced statistical error in the wheel breaking and wheel setting process but did not prevent solutions from being found.

This chapter describes the methods used in the Testery for finding the wheel pin patterns and settings of the S and M wheels: seven wheels in all. With this information known, a Tunny machine could be set up and plaintext in German produced from the ciphertext intercept. The Tunny machine is described in Chapter 10.

The process for finding the S and M wheel pin patterns and setting starts with the pseudo plaintext D (the de-chi tape) produced in the Newmanry plus substantial linguistic skills and statistical information. The process was called "depsiing" or when unsuccessful "deep sighing." Depsiing "was carried out by hand, mostly by members of the W.R.N.S."* [1]

Changes to the X, S, and M wheels were effective on the schedule shown in Table 6.1. This change schedule was not universal, individual links changed on their own schedules. The daily changes were initiated by an originating operator. At some time after midnight a Q code signal would be sent telling the receiving operator that the next message would use the next day's patterns. It was possible that messages would be sent in two directions on the same link using different daily patterns.

Table 6.1 Key Change Schedule

Date	*X* Pin Patterns	*S* Pin Patterns	*M* Pin Patterns	X , S, and M Wheel Setting
Start of use	Monthly	3 Months [2]	Monthly	Each Message
May 1942 [3]	Monthly	3 Months	Daily	Each Message
October 1942 [4]	Monthly	Monthly	Daily	Each Message
July 1944 [5]	Daily	Daily	Daily	Each Message

Finding S Patterns

The first step in the Testery to find the pin patterns of the S wheels begins with finding S'. This process demands more cryptanalysis capability using cribs than mathematics as needed in the Newmanry. Recall from Chapter 4 that $D = P \oplus S'$. In other words, D is the plaintext enciphered by the S' wheels. In delta form, $\Delta D = \Delta P \oplus \Delta S'$. The S wheels do not move on every enciphered character; they are stationary about 70% of the time. Thus about 70% of the time $\Delta S' = 0$. At these times, ΔD bears a strong relationship to ΔP and was frequently equal to ΔP.

---

* Women's Royal Naval Service.

The GCHQ accumulated a large amount of data on German plaintext messages sent over the Fish links. There were significant differences in the statistics for the various links due to the characteristics of the messages transmitted and the habits of the operators assigned to the links. These characteristics are similar to the characteristic "fist" of Morse code operators. A rich source of cribs for stripping *S*' from the pseudo plaintext, *D*, was provided by these statistics.

Albert Small[6] provides statistics on ΔD and ΔP that lends validity to the basic assumption of the relationship of ΔD to ΔP. These data were taken from 3,200 characters of ΔD and 25,600 characters of ΔP.* It can be seen that the characters of ΔP with high representation are frequently the same characters of ΔD even though the frequencies of occurrence are not identical.

Table 6.2 Counts of ΔP and ΔD Characters

Character	ΔP	ΔD	Character	ΔP	ΔD
+	361	143	Y	94	97
/	156	128	A	102	96
U	196	124	P	88	96
3	150	113	I	55	96
8	157	112	V	51	94
9	75	110	R	76	92
O	133	104	L	66	92
S	93	104	C	73	90
J	139	103	4	63	90
H	72	102	Z	82	89
Q	66	101	E	81	89
F	134	100	D	79	89
M	104	100	K	68	89
G	100	100	W	67	89
N	61	100	X	76	87
T	58	99	B	24	82

It was possible that a skilled cryptanalyst could deduce ΔP from ΔD, the pseudo plaintext. Then by integrating ΔP the plaintext would be found. But that was not the goal of the Newmanry at this point. The goal was to find the *K, S,* and *M* pin wheel patterns so that a month's worth of ciphertext messages could be broken, not just a single message.

As with many attacks on the Fish system, delta values yielded the best results. Because of the correspondence between ΔD and ΔP, a crib in ΔP suggested a portion of *P* plaintext text. *S*' could be found because $S' = D \oplus P$. The knowledge of $\Delta S'$ lead to ΔS which was integrated to find *S*, the pin patterns of the *S* wheels.

The GCHQ maintained extensive files of information derived from broken ciphertext messages. Table 6.3, shows some plaintext segments and their occurrences on two links. Each of these collections was from 100,000 characters of plaintext. The cryptanalyst knowing a link identity, recorded by Knockholt, could match the potential cribs to the known characteristics of the link thereby improving the chances of finding good cribs.

* The ΔP data was normalized to 3,200 characters from 25,600 characters.

Table 6.3 Potential Cribs from Two links, Number of Concurrencies
From 100,000 characters of plaintext

Plaintext fragment	Jellyfish	Stickleback	Plaintext fragment	Jellyfish	Stickleback
89R0EM95	61		9ROEM955		83
5M89KD05M8	38		889R0EM955		53
9DG9H0SF95	29		955LL889		51
5M89ROEM89	27		ANGRIFF		32
AVSCHNITT	23		9IM9RAUM9		27
9ANGRIFF	31		88ARMEE55		26
5M89D5M89	20		55M889SUED		24
5M89A5M89	20		SUEDUKRAIN		21
5M89GR5M89	16		GRIUPPE9SUED		20
5M89WEST	34		889PZ55M88		20
TAETIGKEIT	15	16	HEERESGRUPPE		17
AUFKLAERUN	14				
9NACHR5889	15				

Note from these two samples that there are significant differences in the style of these two links. There is only one potential crib that is on both lists, TAETIGKEIT.

There are strong cribs in this data. One of the characteristics of plaintext that is apparent in Table 6.3 is the treatment of the breaks between sentences that can be used as cribs. In Baudot code the period, or full stop, was not one of the primary, lower case, characters in the Teleprinter code. Thus the following sequence of characters was a common sequence used to end a sentence and begin another one.*

Code	Character	Function
11011	5	Figures (UC)
00111	M	Period
11111	8	Letters (LC)
00100	9	Space

This sequence (5 M 8 9) was also sometimes used to mark the end of an abbreviation and is apparent in the Jellyfish potential cribs of Table 6.3. Some originating operators added additional shift changes at the beginning and the end to make sure that shifts had taken place. The following sequence of characters is used in the example message of Figure 5.4.

Code	Character	Function
11011	5	Figures (UC)
11011	5	Figures (UC)
00111	M	Period
11111	8	Letters (LC)
11111	8	Letters (LC)
00100	9	Space

The (8 8 9) sequence is apparent in the Stickleback potential cribs of Table 6.3. These frequently occurring plaintext patterns have very distinctive ΔP (because $\Delta D = \Delta P$

* If "Period" and "Space" had been assigned to lower case, this characteristic would have been subdued and these highly characteristic cribs would not have been available.

about 60% of the time) patterns that help the cryptanalysts tease out the plaintext and wheel pin patterns of a message. Four examples of plaintext cribs that were known by GCHQ in their ΔP form are shown below.* [7]

Example	Plaintext	Plaintext	ΔP Crib
1	Figures (UC) • Letters (LC) Space	5M89	UA5
2	Figures (UC) – Letters (LC) Space	5A89	OM5
3	Letters (LC) Space ROEM Figures (UC) • Letters (LC) Space	89R0EM5M89	5CLBXUUA5
4	VER	VER	8J

From a printed de-chi tape *D*, ΔD can be computed by a cryptanalyst. A special machine, Junior, is described in Chapter 10 that printed the de-chi tape off-line from a Colossus. The following example is taken from the "Report on British Attack on Fish."[8] The process of finding *S*' begins with ΔD and *D*.

```
ΔD =   8 5 C X I B U 8 U O T 3 L / Q
 D =  V E G H D K P Z C D Z E 5 5 A H
```

The digraph 5C, in ΔD above, was identified as a possible crib into ΔP and a guess was made that it was the Δ of 89R, of the plaintext 89ROEM5M89.† This plaintext crib 89ROEM5M89 was called the tentative plaintext.

```
ΔD = 8 5 C X I B U 8 U O T 3 L / Q
D = V E G H D K P Z C D Z E 5 5 A H
P    = 8 9 R O E M 5 M 8 9 (tentative)
S'   = V V V Z C R R L P Y (tentative)
```

There was now a guess of a tentative fragment of *P*. For this fragment, a fragment of *S*' can be computed by $S' = P \oplus D$. For example: E ⊕ 8 = V, G ⊕ 9 = V, and so on.‡ This process continues until a tentative fragment of *S*' was found, V V V Z C R R L P Y.

By piecing together short sequences using cribs for both the stylized endings described above and German plaintext,§ the entire sequence of *P* and *S*' could be constructed by a skilled cryptanalyst. At this point, the solution was no longer called tentative but probable.

However, what was wanted was *S* not *S*' because *S* was needed to set up a Tunny for deciphering other ciphertext messages. The S' found above, VVVZCRRLPY, can be interpreted as follows. At some point, reading from the left, *S'* has the Baudot code for V. For the next two steps the *S* wheels did not advance and *S*' remains V. The next advance of the *S* wheel produced Z, the next C, then R, L, P, and Y. This analysis gives a strongly probable estimate of the pin patterns for a portion of the *S* wheel:

* The meaning of ROEM and VER is not known but believed to be abbreviations used in military plaintext.

† See Chapter 10 for a description of DRAGON, a machine for registering cribs on the de-chi, or *D* tape.

‡ See Figure 3.11.

§ Such as SUEDUKRAIN in Table 6.3.

S = V Z C R L P Y.

There was only a small probability that double pairs, such as R R, are the result of two characters in sequence on the *S* wheels. As discussed in Chapter 9, the Germans made a special effort that these patterns were not used.

The number of pins on each of the *S* wheels was known, thus simplifying the search for the *S* wheel pin patterns. As character patterns are discovered, the pin patterns of the individual *S* wheels can be established. Recall that the lengths of the *S* wheels are: 43, 47, 51, 53, and 59. Thus only relatively short sequences of *S* were needed to completely determine the pin patterns.*

The unique idea behind this method for breaking the *S* wheels was that the cribs are found in ΔD not D as might be expected. The use of differences was a very powerful tool. Further, at this stage of the process the full characters were used, not one or two channels as had been the case with *X* wheel setting.

Wheel Setting

After the five *S* wheel pin patterns had been discovered, it was necessary to find the setting and make the correspondence to the indicators. Clearly for the ciphertext message that was used to find the *S* wheel pin patterns the setting was known. However, a technique was needed for setting other messages that are sent on the same day but with different *S* wheel settings.

Finding the settings of the *S* wheels was an exercise in pure cryptography; few machine aids were devised to assistance in this task. In general, the approach was to set one *S* wheel at a time, working with full characters did not yield results. Recall that the de-chi tape or pseudo plaintext, *D*, was available. And the pin patterns for the *S* wheels were found as described above. As seen in Chapter 4:

$D = P \oplus S'$.

and

$P = D \oplus S'$

What was done was that D and S' were added (mod2) together for all settings of S'_5 (59 possible starting positions) and the fifth channel of P was examined.† In other words, $P_5 = D_5 \oplus S'_5$. A count was made of $P_5 = 0$ for each of the 59 settings. The largest count is the correct setting and was much sharper than with *X* wheel setting using the Double Delta Algorithm.[9]

Another test used wheels 1 and 4 of the D and S'. For this test, 2,279 settings must be evaluated and the test was to count the tokens $P_1 \oplus P_4 = 0$. There was some evidence that a Colossus was used for this test. However, the Channel 5 wheel setting test was done by manual means.

---

* The cycle of the *S* wheels is 3.22×10^8 so a complete S cycle will never be seen

† It is not clear from the record as to why channel 5 was selected. Probably channel 5 of typical German plaintext gave a sharper indication of the correct setting.

Motor Wheel Breaking and Setting

As with the other wheels, the motor wheels had to be broken for ciphertext using the same key and set for each message. The procedures for accomplishing this are discussed in the following paragraphs.

Remember that the *S* wheels step under the control of the motor wheels. Finding the pin patterns of the motor wheels would be a relatively straight forward task given that the difference between *S*' and *S* was known. That is, the time at which S steps, signifying a pin set to a 1, can be resolved by observing the pattern of *S*' as shown previously.

However, the problem was far more difficult due to limitations used by the Germans and discussed in Chapter 9 and their effect needs mentioning here. Limitations introduce additional stepping of the *S* wheel depending upon a prior state of an *X* wheel and/or a prior state of a *Z* channel. These additional steps of the *S* wheels required great cryptanalysis skills to unravel. But this was done at GCHQ.

Setting the motor wheels were required for each message after the *X*, *S* and *M* wheel pin patterns known. There were two methods used for setting the *M* wheels.

The first method essentially was to break a ciphertext message from the beginning, finding each of the wheel patterns (*X*, *S*, and *M*) and the settings for *X* and *S*. A solution to the setting of the *M* wheels was fitted in by trial and error so that the solution was obtained. Clearly this was a task for a skilled cryptanalyst.

The second method was to set the motor wheels on a Colossus. [10] For this method, ΔD of a ciphertext message was required. Table 6.2 shows the relative frequency of occurrence of various ΔD characters: + and / being very frequent. Experimentation showed that the occurrence of these characters was more pronounced when the motor wheels were set than otherwise.

There are 37×61 = 2,257 possible settings of the motor wheels. A Colossus would be set up to make a frequency count of these interesting ΔD characters with each of the 2,257 motor wheel settings. There was a very sharp indication of the correct motor wheel settings.

It is not clear from the contemporary reports if motor wheel setting with Colossus was routinely employed or if the manual method was preferred. The inference can be made that, as Colossus time was needed for *X* wheel breaking and setting, the manual method was preferred.

Finding Plaintext

Once the wheel pin patterns for a day's traffic on a link and wheel settings for the individual messages were known, the messages could be deciphered on Tunny. This machine, an analog of the Lorenz machine, is described in Chapter 10.

The output of Tunny was German plaintext and the plaintext had to be translated before the results were useful. At that stage of the process, there would be garbles that must be removed and some interpretation of the plaintext would have been needed. For example, unusual abbreviations might have to be expanded and references to prior messages added.

References

[1]Tutte, W., "Fish and I", http://frode.home.cern.ch/frode/crypto/tutte.html, pg, 8.
[2] Michie, D., Good, J., Timms, G., *General Report on Tunny*, 1945, Released to the Public Record Office in 2000, http://www.alanturing.net/tunny_report, pg 320.
[3] (ibid.. 308).
[4] (ibid. 320).
[5] (ibid. 319).
[6] Small, A. *Special Fish Report,* NARA, NR 4628 Box 1417, also http://www.codesandciphter.org.uk/documents/small/page112.htm, December 1944, pg. 4-5.
[7] Anonymous, *Report on British Attack on "FISH",* Communications Intelligence Technical Paper TS 47, Navy Department, Washington D.C., May 1945, RG 457, Box 607, pg. 81.
[8] (ibid. 81).
[9] (ibid. 83).
[10] (ibid. 92).

Chapter 7

Robinson Machines

Background

Wheel breaking and wheel setting by hand proved to be successful but labor intensive. As wheel pin patterns were good for one month (until the change period was changed to each day in July 1944), mechanization of wheel setting was needed first because wheel settings were unique to each message.

Two classes of machines were developed to mechanize the processes at GCHQ. These were Robinsons and Colossi. The Robinsons served as research and prototyping machines that gave valuable insight into the design of the faster and more useful Colossi. This chapter discusses the Robinson machines; Colossi are discussed in Chapter 8.

Keep in mind that wheel setting is a statistical process and the fundamental requirement for Robinsons and Colossi was that they be counting machines. That is, the machines must count the logical outcome of various binary combinations of bits in the ciphertext and keytext streams. Every component of Robinsons supported this counting function.

For a ciphertext message of 10,000 characters, the number of double delta calculations will be $1{,}271\times 10{,}000 = 12{,}710{,}000$. Moreover, as each double delta calculation requires seven Boolean operations, the total process required over 88 million $\oplus$ operations. This number of operations effectively removed the double delta technique from consideration if done by hand.

Tutte approached Major Morgan, the Head of Research[1] and Max Newman, the leader of the Newmanry, to discuss the possibility of a machine aid for performing the double delta algorithm.[2] In December 1942, the decision to design a machine for the double delta algorithm was made with the first machine scheduled for delivery in June 1943.[3] [4] A group of skilled telephone equipment designers worked at the Telecommunications Research Establishment (TRE) and this talent was enlisted to design and produce this machine aid.[5] The first machine, named Heath Robinson[*] was delivered in April 1943;[6] no photograph of Heath Robinson is known to exist. The lead designer is believed to be F. O. Morrell.[7]

There were at least three versions of the Robinson machines, Heath Robinson, Old Robinson, and Super Robinson.[†] [8] There were also Double Robinsons, some completed and some under construction. These machines had four paper tape readers, called bedsteads, rather than the two on other machines.[9]

One of the major contributors to the design of Robinson was C. E. Wynn-Williams who had designed high-speed counters in the 1930s for atomic research.[10] In

---

[*] Heath Robinson was a British cartoonist who drew fanciful machines similar to the U.S. cartoonist Rube Goldberg.

[†] Bryan Randell writes that there were four named, Heath Robinson, Peter Robinson, Robinson, and Cleaver. The evidence indicates that each was a unique machine; serial production of any did not take place. Cleaver may have been Colossus MK I.

addition to this background, Wynn-Williams was a creative circuit designer and created an innovative Xor circuit that was critical to the double delta algorithm execution on Robinson.

The major conceptual design problem for both Robinsons and Colossi was what to use for memory. Fish ciphertext messages were characterized by large data sets that had to be handled and processed. In the 1940s, only two technologies were available to the designers of a large memory, punched paper tape and IBM punched cards. For the TRE designers, punched paper tape was the memory of choice. This was the media of teleprinter communications thus the media that was most familiar to the telephone engineers who designed the machines.* Therefore, the selection of punched paper tape memory set the tone for the entire design project.

Robinsons were designed by telephone engineers who used standard telephone hardware wherever possible. The second machine in the series, Old Robinson, shown in Figure 7.1 was constructed on three standard telephone frames or racks holding standard panels.[11] There are three frames were: one for the paper tape readers called "bedsteads" with their electronics, one frame for the counters (and later the printer), and one frame for the logic circuits with a jack panel. Telephone cables interconnected the logic circuits to program a particular algorithm. † The box-like item on a table to the right is a Gifford printer, discussed later in this chapter. [12]

Figure 7.1 Old Robinson
(The National Archives, London)

* It should be noted that both the U.S. Army and Navy cryptographic services made a different choice. They chose IBM cards for memory and used modified standard IBM equipment to support their activities. Jack Good reports that the BP personnel working of Enigma traffic used punched card equipment for sorting to find tetragraphs and pentagraphs, pg. 156, *Codebreakers*.

† The ENIAC, developed at the Moore School, was programmed by patching the computational components into the algorithm.

Each Robinson was an upgrade on the previous model. The Robinson class machines gave valuable design insight for the design of Colossus. In May 1945, only two Robinsons are listed as operational, with two nearly complete.[13] Some of the early Robinson class machines must have been retired as new ones became operational. Alternatively, a more likely case is that the design of Colossus was progressing so well that only two or three Robinsons were ever built. None of the circuits designed for Robinson found their way into the Colossus design. Tommy Flowers, the designer of Colossus, believed that the Robinson circuits were unsuitable for a refined processor and started with a clean sheet of paper for all of the circuits, a topic discussed in Chapter 8.[14]

The time line of Figure 7.2 shows the important dates for the Robinson machines. Designers of complex computational equipment will recognize the Herculean effort made by the designers of this equipment. This effort was mounted before the advent of computers and computer aided design tools.

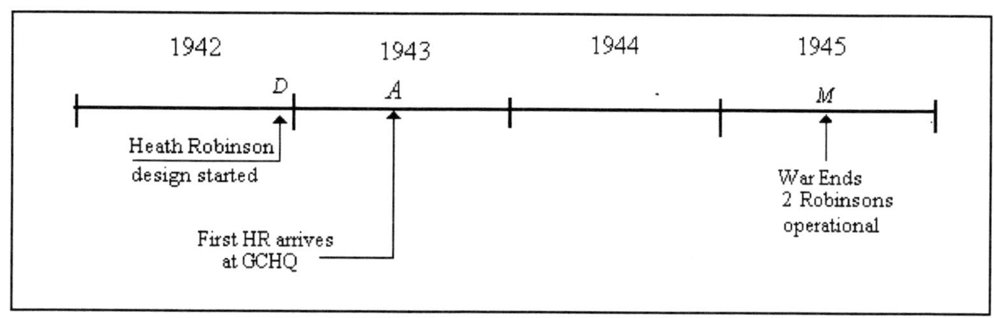

Figure 7.2 Robinson Machines Time Line

Old Robinson Design

Major problems exist today in determining design details of Old Robinson. Only one photograph is known to survive that shows its construction, Figure 7.1. Some word descriptions in some of the surviving documents and one circuit diagram have been uncovered by Tony Sale. Allen Coombs, one of the Robinson designers, described some circuits with diagrams in 1983. [15] Sale has interviewed some of the surviving designers and has started the construction of a Heath Robinson replica. Because of the paucity of information, a number of assumptions have to be made to present the following description of this machine.

One of the major functions of the Robinson machines, and Colossi as well, is the handling of punched paper tape. It is instructive to look at the tape itself, shown in Figure 7.3. The tape containing the ciphertext is spliced into an endless loop by pasting together the two ends of the tape. The joint overlap covers two sprocket holes. The blank portion is without punches except for the start and stop punches.

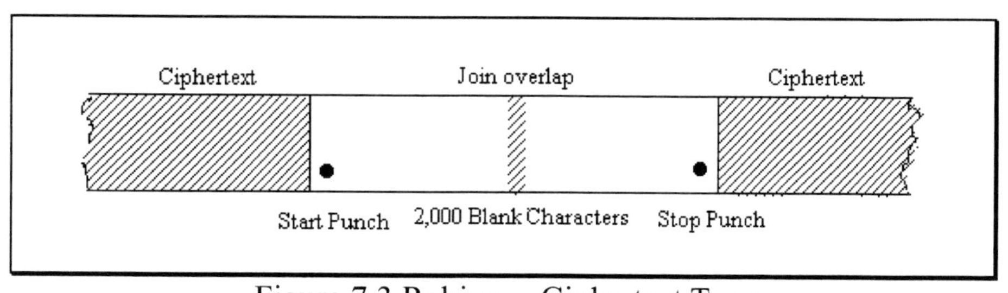

Figure 7.3 Robinson Ciphertext Tape

A start punch and a stop punch reset and synchronize the processing equipment.[16] A minimum of 2,000 blank characters separate the Start/Stop punches and the ciphertext data.[17] At 2,000 characters per second, the time available for relays to respond and for synchronization is approximately one second.

A block diagram of Old Robinson is shown in Figure 7.4. The data on each of the two tapes is read by photoelectric tape readers and processed by the logic system and displayed on indicator lights or printed. Another counter counts sprocket holes on the Cipher Tape to indicate the wheel setting under examination. The ciphertext and keytext streams were read from two punched paper tapes into the logic section where various operations were performed and sent to the counters to give scores.

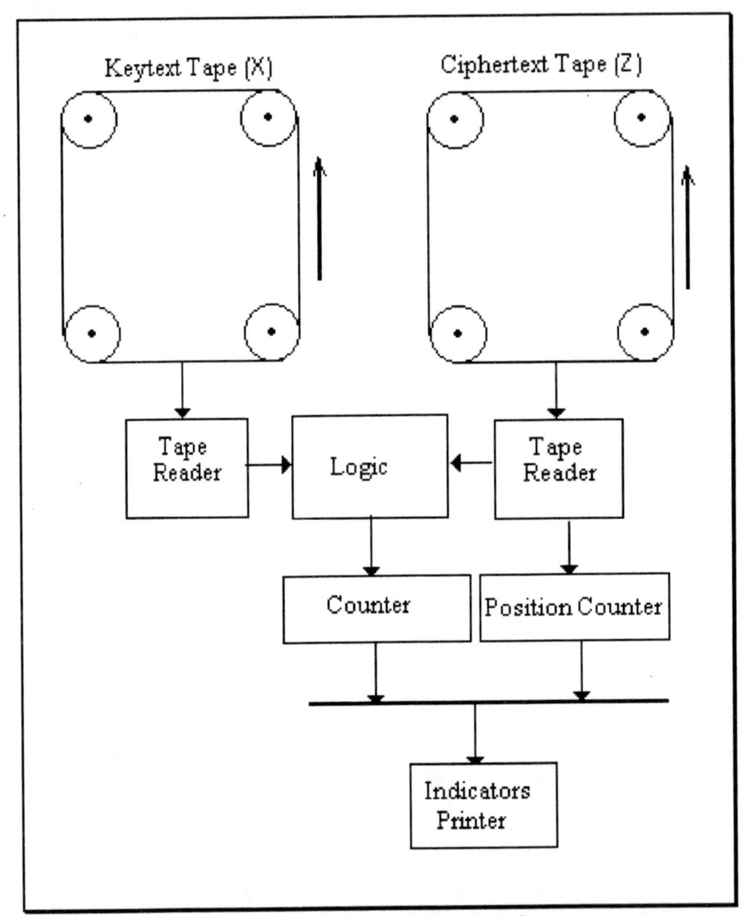

Figure 7.4 Robinson Block Diagram

Wheel Setting on Old Robinson

The process of wheel setting is illustrated with an example; the ciphertext stream (*Z*) has twelve characters and the keytext stream (*X*) has four characters. The keytext stream is replicated so that it matches the length of the ciphertext. The replicated keytext stream is passed three times past the ciphertext stream. This example is similar, but smaller, to the wheel setting example of Chapter 4, Figures 4.3 and 4.5. Although this example speaks of "characters", the actual implementation of wheel setting is performed on two bits of the keytext and ciphertext as described in Chapter 4.

To aid in the description of the double delta algorithm's implementation the algorithm is at first represented by (Op). Op processes each pair of Δ keytext and Δ ciphertext characters. The output of each (Op), called a token, is either a one or zero; the zeros tokens are counted to give the score of the twelve terms. Each pass accumulates the zero tokens that are used to discover the most probable wheel setting of the key. After each pass, the key is shifted one character position relative to the ciphertext and the process repeats.[*] This process can be better understood by referring to Figure 4.2.

Cipher *Z* 01 02 03 04 05 06 07 08 09 10 11 12
Key *X* 01 02 03 04 01 02 03 04 01 02 03 04

Pass 1

Score = (*Z*01 op *X*01) + (*Z*02 op *X*02) + (*Z03* op *X*03) + (*Z*04 op *X*04) [†]
+ (*Z*05 op *X*01) + (*Z*06 op *X*02) + (*Z*07 op *X*03) + (*Z*08 op *X*04)
+ (*Z*09 op *X*01) + (*Z*10 op *X*02) + (*Z*11 op *X*03) + (*Z*12 op *X*04)

Pass 2

Cipher. *Z* 01 02 03 04 05 06 07 08 09 10 11 12
SHIFT *X* 1 place 04 01 02 03 04 01 02 03 04 01 02 03

Score = (*Z*01 op *X*04) + (*Z*02 op *X*01) +...+ (*Z*12 op *X*03)

Pass 3

Cipher. *Z* 01 02 03 04 05 06 07 08 09 10 11 12
SHIFT *X* 1 place 03 04 01 02 03 04 01 02 03 04 01 02

Score = (*Z*01 op *X*03) + (*Z*02 op *X*04) +...+ (*Z*12 op *X*02)

Pass 4

Cipher. *Z* 01 02 03 04 05 06 07 08 09 10 11 12
SHIFT *X* 1 place 02 03 04 01 02 03 04 01 02 03 04 01

Score = (*Z*01 op *X*02) + (*Z*02 op *X*03) +...+ (*Z*12 op *X*01)

Each score is displayed and/or printed. The pass with the largest score (most zeros) indicates the probable wheel setting of the keytext. For example if the score is largest for pass 3, *Z*01 was enciphered with *X*03; *Z*02 was enciphered with *X*04, etc.

---

[*] Shifting was accomplished by adding a null character at the end of the cipher tape.
[†] The + symbol represents counting the tokens.

The approximate time required for finding the X_1 and X_2 wheel setting by this method is:

$$\text{Time} \approx (\text{Length of Z} \times \text{Length of X}) \div \text{Tape character rate.}^*$$

The example above requires 4 × 12 = 48 time steps. For a ciphertext message of 10,000 characters, a keytext of 1,271 characters, and the tapes streaming at 2,000 characters per second, the approximate time to perform X_1 and X_2 wheel setting on Robinson was 1.8 hours. Because of 2,000 blank characters on the tapes that reduce the effective processing rate, a more accurate approximation is 2.1 hours.

Bedstead Paper Tape Readers

Because of the great length of the tapes, the engineers developed a concept they named "bedsteads." For a 10,000-character ciphertext message, the tape would be approximately 100 feet in length. Tapes of this length could not be handled if they were allowed to fall free on the floor; some kind of handling mechanism was needed. A key tape of 1,271 characters would be approximately 9 feet in length. However, several copies of the keytext were punched into one tape so that the keytext tape is approximately the same length as the ciphertext tape.[18] †

The bedsteads held very long tapes in a serpentine arrangement that permitted the tapes to be advanced at a high velocity over the two photoelectric tape readers. The tapes passed over a number of wheels that were used to hold the long tape and maintain tension. The original Heath Robinson carried both the ciphertext and keytext messages on one bedstead frame.[19] The design of the two-tape drive arrangement that synchronized the two tapes is shown in Figure 7.5.

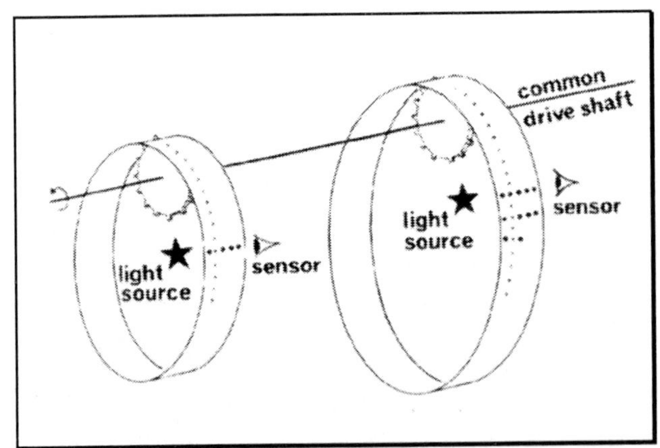

Figure 7.5 Loop Tapes
(© 1983 IEEE)

* This performance model is first developed in Chapter 4.

† The question of the length of the ciphertext tape is not clear. Flowers implies that the key tape was short and made more revolutions through the reader than the ciphertext tape. However, it can be assumed that both techniques were the subject of experimentation.

The tapes were driven by their sprocket holes from a common drive shaft that insured that the tapes remained in synchronization as the double delta calculations were performed. After each pass over the cipher tape, the counted tally was displayed or printed. An operator scanned the printed tally score values and was able to uncover the start point of the key tape.

The practice of driving the two tapes from a common drive shaft was later modified so that the tapes were driven by friction rollers and the common shaft maintained synchronization between the two tapes.[20]

The five channels of the paper tape were illuminated with a light shinning through a mask, Figure 7.6,* before striking the photoelectric detectors. The mask was patterned so that the light hitting the photo detectors was as near as possible a square wave as the round tape holes passed by. The two rows of five large openings corresponded to the five data channels of the tape, see Figure 1.1, and the small half-mask corresponds to the sprocket hole channel. Reading the sprocket holes provided the synchronization pulses for the electronics of Robinson. Also, note that two characters are read simultaneously to provide inputs of the ith and i+1bits to the double delta process.

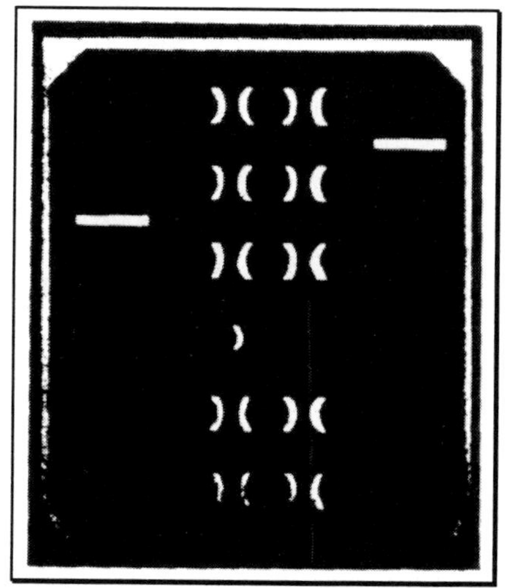

Figure 7.6 Paper Tape Mask
(© 1983 IEEE)

Notice in Figure 7.6 that there were 23 apertures, 20 for the five channels, one for the sprocket hole and two rectangular ones to read "start" and "stop" punches in the tape. These punches started and terminated the counting process.

The bedstead concept was successful and carried over to the Colossus machines. However, the reliability of Robinson was marginal; the tapes were always giving trouble. Due to the high speed of the tapes and the number of passes that had to be made to find the wheel setting, tape stretching was a problem. While sprockets that were driven from a common shaft drove the two tapes, skew problems developed at the reading stations. Correcting this problem was a major design goal for Colossus.

* A number of photographs of this mask, each different, have been published. There probably was an evolution in the mask design leading up to the mask used on Colossus.

Robinson Processing Circuits

Wynn-Williams had extensive experience in the pre-war years with electronic circuits. Thus it was natural that when presented with the design problem of implementing the double delta algorithm that he would search for an electronic solution. The required speed made any other technology, such as relay logic unusable. Four Robinson circuits are discussed in the following paragraphs. Figure 7.7 is the original circuit diagram for Heath Robinson dated July 17, 1943.*

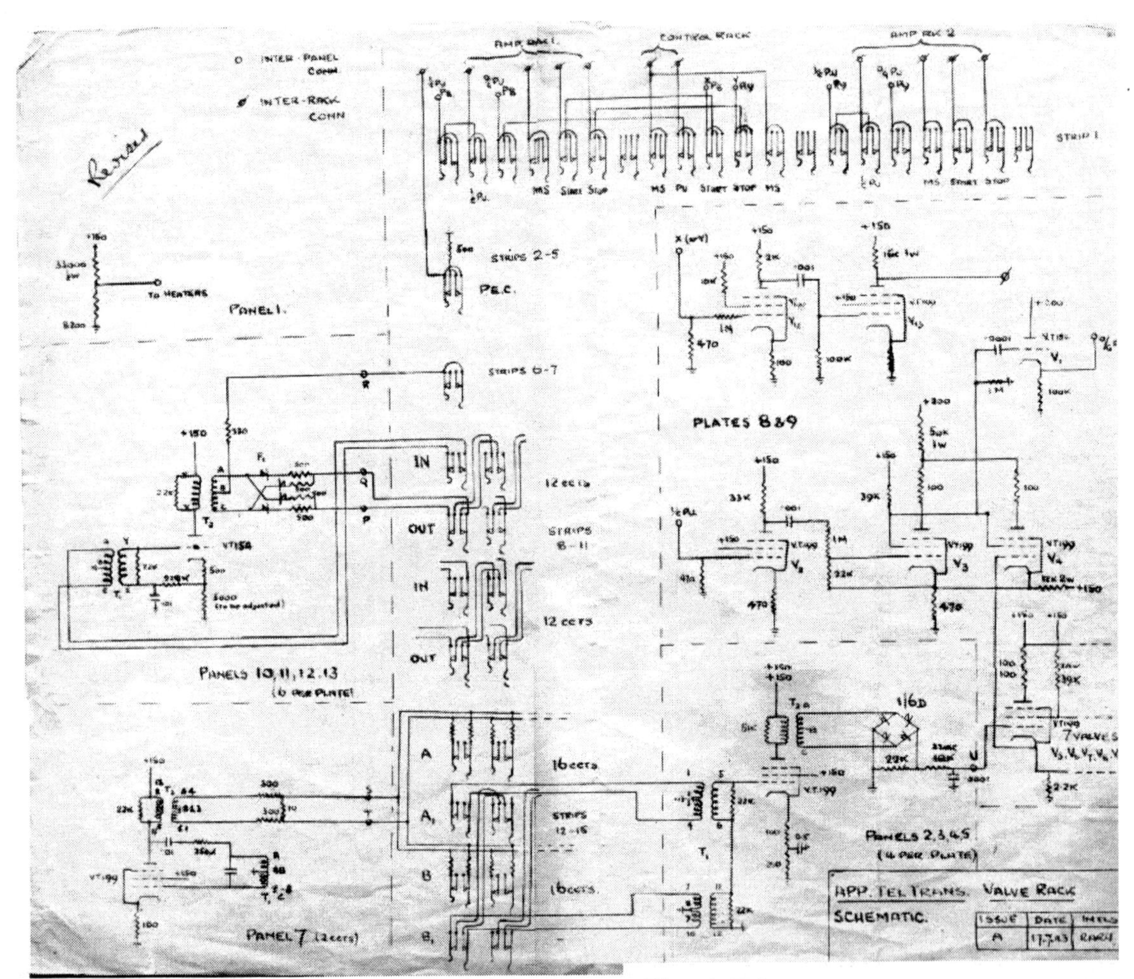

Figure 7.7 Heath Robinson Circuit Diagram
(Courtesy of Tony Sale)

Xor Circuits

Tape speed was limited to about 2,000 characters per second, approximately 12 Miles per Hour, due to tape driving and synchronization problems. Thus the seven Boolean operations of the double delta algorithm had to be performed in 0.5 msec. Executing this many Boolean operations in such a short time was a rather remarkable achievement for the technology of the day.

* Tony Sale recovered the circuit diagram for Heath Robinson that was retained by one of the designers. This diagram was post dated after the delivery of Heath Robinson.

Recall from Chapter 4 that the tokens for Channels 1 and 2 were found by,

$$\text{Token}_i = \Delta X_1 \oplus \Delta X_2 \oplus \Delta Z_1 \oplus \Delta Z_2$$
$$= X_{1,1} \oplus X_{1,2} \oplus X_{2,1} \oplus X_{2,2} \oplus Z_{1,1} \oplus Z_{1,2} \oplus Z_{2,1} \oplus Z_{2,2}$$

In other words, a token is the Xor of eight bits giving a one or a zero.* Wynn-Williams designed an Xor circuit using phase shift from a reference oscillator to convey a one or zero. Zero was represented by 0^0 phase shift; a one was represented by a phase shift of 180^0. With this design $1 \oplus 1 = 0$, $180^0 + 180^0 = 0^0$. Likewise, $0 \oplus 1 = 1$, $0^0 + 180^0 = 180^0$, exactly what was wanted.

The diagram of the Xor or mod2 adder circuit is shown in Figure 7.8. The Master Oscillator, indicated as B, oscillates at 25kc/s and feeds the first A circuit. The output of the first A stage (either shifted 180^0 or $0^{0)}$ is the reference input to the second A stage, and so on. Thus the reference signal is progressively shifted, or not shifted, in phase in each A stage.

A caption in the figure is misleading. One A stage is not a full mod2 adder; it is only one half of such an adder. Two A stages are required to form the Xor of two inputs.

The final logic stage drives the Comparator Circuit and Output circuit. The output of the last mod2 adders is compared to the reference frequency from the master oscillator, addition is performed by the two input transformers. If the frequencies are in phase, they add, and if out of phase, they cancel. The resulting signal is rectified and a binary signal is produced that is the mod2 sum of all of the inputs.

These circuits gave significant troubles.[21] With the tape reader sensing ones or zeros at 2,000 per second, there were less than 10 cycles of the master oscillator for all of the logic operations to be performed and the logic output generated. At some point, a decision was made to adopt a new Xor circuit for the Colossus, described in Chapter 8.

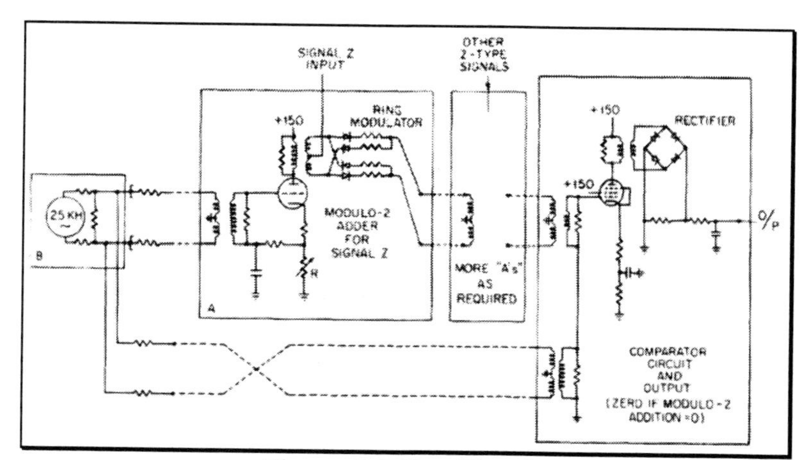

Figure 7.8 Xor Circuits
(© 1983 IEEE)

Figure 7.9 illustrates how these circuits were used. Two of the Phase Shifters combine to give an Xor circuit. The first Phase Shifter receives an input from the Oscillator and one of the DC logic values from the X or Z paper tapes. The second Phase

* This is the identical operation for computing parity.

Shifter receives the output of the first Phase Shifter and a second DC logic value. By cascading the Phase Shifters, the Xor of the DC logic values is produced.

At the end of the cascaded Phase Shifters, the Output Amplifier combines the two 25 kHz signals and produces a DC logic value that is the Xor of the DC inputs. For the case of generating the score of the double delta algorithm, there are sixteen of these Phase Shifters in cascade.

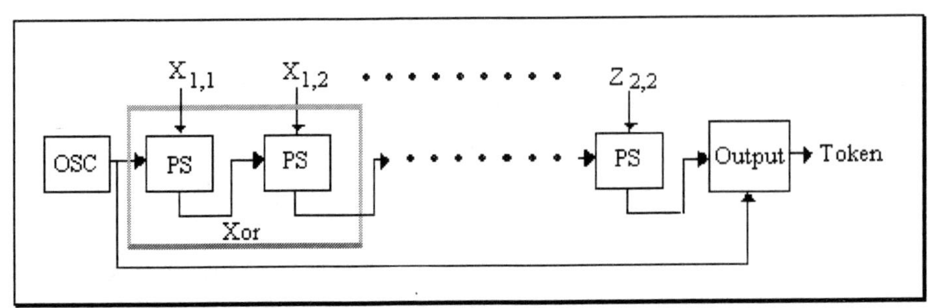

Figure 7.9 Cascaded Xor Circuits for Token

All indications from Figure 7.7 suggest that there were 24 Phase Shifters and 16 Output Amplifiers. However, 16 Phase Shifters and 1 Output Amplifier are required to perform the double delta algorithm on two channels and produce the token. Three channels would require an additional 10 Phase shifters and one Output Amplifier. If double delta is performed on all five channels, 22 Phase Shifters and 5 Output Amplifiers are needed. There were a number of algorithms patched up on Robinson, not just wheel setting, that use the Xor circuits.

Programming the algorithm consisted of plugging the various circuits together by means of the plug board and cables. As shown in Figure 7.7, there were 15 20-plug standard telephone plug strips.

1 Strip	Inputs from Paper Tape Amplifiers and synchronization signals
4 Strips	PEC*
2 Strips	Logic inputs to Phase Shifters
4 Strips	Inputs and Outputs to/from Phase Shifters
4 Strips	Distribution of Master Oscillator and Inputs to Output Amplifiers

Photocell Amplifier Circuit

Figure 7.10 shows the photocell amplifier that was designed by Arnold Lynch in 1942.[22] Michie, Good, and Timms write that Heath Robinson "could not tolerate long stretches of dots or of crosses."[23] This comment is confirmed by the fact that the photocell amplifiers were AC coupled by capacitors as shown in Figure 7.10.†

---

* Use not understood.

† Tony Sale found the same phenomena with his construction of a Colossus replica. As discussed in Chapter 8 he made modifications to the photocell masks that reduced or eliminated the problem.

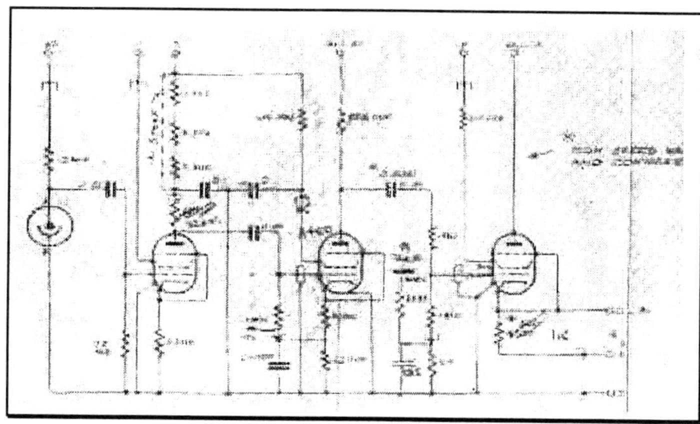

Figure 7.10 Photocell Amplifier
(Courtesy of Tony Sale)

Decade Counters

The zero tokens, as they emerge from the logic cascade, were counted; the counters in effect performed a summation. The maximum number of counts, for one evaluation of double delta of channels 1 and 2, is the number of characters of the ciphertext. For a ciphertext of 10,000 characters, four decades of counters are required that count form 0 to 9,999. Although the most probable count is 0.55 × the ciphertext length, four decades are still required. With the tape streaming at 2,000 characters per second and a 10,000-character ciphertext, a score was completed every 5 seconds.

In addition to counting the tokens, the position of the tape must also be counted as shown in Figure 7.4 in order to identify the wheel setting associated with each score. Actually, this counter counted the revolutions of the ciphertext tape requiring that the actual position be computed, a source of errors.[24]

The design of the counters has been discovered by Tony Sale in his project to reconstruct a Heath Robinson.[25] The first decade (least significant decade) was an electronic counter that must respond and tally a pulse every 1/2000th of a second or every 0.5 millisecond. The high-speed decade of the counter was designed by Wynn-Williams and consisted of ten thyratrons, gas-filled triode tubes, commonly used as rectifiers configured as a ring counter. Tony Sale reports that Harry Fensom, a Heath Robinson designer, says that the counter design was similar to that designed by Wynn-Williams in 1931.[26]

The next two decades of the counters were implemented with high-speed relays while the last decade used slow speed relays. The second decade had a maximum counting period of 1/200th of a second, the third decade, 1/20th of a second and the third, 1/2 second. These are reasonable requirements for relay counters.

As noted previously, there were four of these counters. One pair was used to count tokens and record the score. The other pair of counters was used to count the ciphertext tape sprocket position associated with the score. When the first score had been counted, the logic was switched to a second counter pair and operators read and recorded the score from the first pair. After the next cycle, the logic returned to the first counter pair and the second counter pair was read and recorded. The reason for the two counter pairs was to give the operators time to record a score and a ciphertext tape position as processing continued. With a score every 5 seconds, 5 seconds was available for recording.

The position counter (counts sprocket holes to indicate the liner position of a keytext tape) can be modified by switches to count in special ways. In the normal mode, the counter counts from 0 to 9,999. The counter can be split so that each half is a counter counting from 0 to 99. The counter can also be switched so that two digits show the remainder of the location divided by 41 and the other shows the remainder divided by 31.[27] Thus these two counters show the positions of the *X*1, *X*2 wheels in the cycle of 1,271. In other words, these two counter point to the axis' of the rectangle and direct the Z⊕ tokens to the correct counter for rectangling. It is not known at this time how the counters were forced into the sequences of 41 and 31..

Observing and Recording Scores

With Heath Robinson and Old Robinson, the tally and keytext tape position counts were displayed as they occurred. As can be appreciated, manual recording was a constant source of errors and usually two operators would record the scores in an attempt to reduce the errors.

With Super Robinson, although the displays were retained, a printer augmented them. The details of the printer are not known, however it is reported that a Gifford Printer was used.[28] The designers believed that this printer would be more appropriate for this application than an electric typewriter because the Gifford Printer printed eight digits at once (some form of line printer?). However, the Gifford Printer was never satisfactory; it had many problems, such as indistinct printing, which could not be overcome.

Robinson Upgrades

There are references in the literature to a number of upgrades to the basic Robinson design. For example, a Double Robinson of which two were built had four bedsteads. [29] Another upgrade to the Robinson was made late in the war that added 750 tubes. [30] There is no reliable indication as to the exact purpose of these tubes.

However, I guess that a first model of the electronic key ring generators, later used on Colossus may have been added. This addition would eliminate the major source of problems with Robinson, namely the problems with two tapes. And, as an electronic key ring generator requires approximately 500 tubes, this is a likely candidate.

References

[1] E-mail communications with Bill Tutte and Tony Sale. 2001.
[2] Tutte, W., "FISH and I" University of Waterloo, June 19, 1998.
http://frode.home.cern.ch/frode/crypto/tutte.html, pg. 7.
[3] Michie, D., Good, J., Timms, G., *General Report on Tunny*, 1945, Released to the Public Record Office in 2000, http://www.alanturing.net/tunny_report. Pg. 276.
[4] (Ibid. 308).
[5] Flowers, T., "The Design of Colossus", *The Annals of the History of Computing*, Vol. 5, Number 3, July 1983, pg. 243.
[6] (Michie, *General Report,* 276).
[7] (Flowers, The Design, 243).
[8] Randell, B. R., *The Origins of Digital Computers, Selected Papers,* Springer-Verlag, New York, 1982, pg. 350.

[9] Small, A. *Special Fish Report,* NARA, NR 4628 Box 1417, also http://www.codesandciphter.org.uk/documents/small/page112.htm, December 1944, pg. 108.
[10] Wynn-Williams, C. E., "The Use of Thyratrons for High Speed Automatic Counting of Physical Phenomena", *The Proceeding of the Royal Society of London*, 132, 819, 295-310, July 1, 1931.
[11] e-mail Tony Sale, July 12, 2002.
[12] e-mail Tony Sale, July 12, 2002.
[13] (Michie, *General Report,,* 327).
[14] e-mail Tony Sale, July 12, 2002.
[15] Coombs, A., "The Making of Colossus," *The Annals of the History of Computing*, Vol. 5, Number 3, July 1983, pp. 253-258.
[16] (Michie, *General Report*, 285).
[17] Small, A. *Special Fish Report,* NARA, NR 4628 Box 1417, also http://www.codesandciphter.org.uk/documents/small/page112.htm, December 1944, pg.96.
[18] (Michie, *General Report*, 286). 286.
[19] (Small, *Special Fish*, 107).
[20] e-mail Toney Sale, July 12, 2002.
[21] (Coombs, The Making, 254).
[22] http://www.codesandciphers.org.uk/virtualbp/vcolossus/colpcis_files/col4max.htm.
[23] (Michie, *General Report*, 328).
[24] (ibid, 328).
[25] Sale, A.E., "The Rebuild of Heath Robinson". http://www.qufaro.demon.co.uk/hrob/hrrbldo1.htm, 2001.
[26] Wynn-Williams, C. E. "The Use of Thyratrons for High Speed Automatic Counting of Physical Phenomena", *Proceedings of the Royal Society, Series A* .Vol. 132, Issue 819, July 1931, pg. 299.
[27] (Michie, *General Report*, 356).
[28] Sale, A.E., "The Rebuild of Heath Robinson" http://www.qufaro.demon.co.uk/hrob/hrrbldo1.htm, 2001.
[29] (Small, *Special Fish*, 108).
[30] Anonymous, *Report on British Attack on "FISH",* Communications Intelligence Technical Paper TS 47, Navy Department, Washington D.C., May 1945, NARA RG 457, Box 607, Pg. 49.

Chapter 8

Colossus

Background

Functional limitations and potential reliability problems with Robinson were apparent during its development. Therefore an ambitious development project was initiated in February 1943 that would overcome the deficiencies of Robinson and, in retrospect, bring cryptanalysis into the age of digital computer technology.

The Post Office Research Establishment at Dollis Hill was contacted for help and Max Newman talked to Tommy Flowers about the desire for a faster, more robust machine than Robinson. Flowers had experience with electronic circuits and proposed an electronic solution to the design problem presented to him by Newman. The first Colossus, Colossus MK I, was operational in January 1944 and installed in the Newmanry in February 1944. The first MK II followed in June 1944.

Figure 8.1 shows two views of a Colossus. The right view shows two bedsteads. One would hold a ciphertext tape being processed; the second would be in the process of having a tape mounted for an upcoming run. Also, an IBM Electromatic typewriter is shown on a stand with a shelf behind holding plugs and switches for rectangling, (described later in this chapter). The left view shows the two racks, separated by about ten feet for maintenance and adjustments. The large box-like items on the left frame are the power supplies.

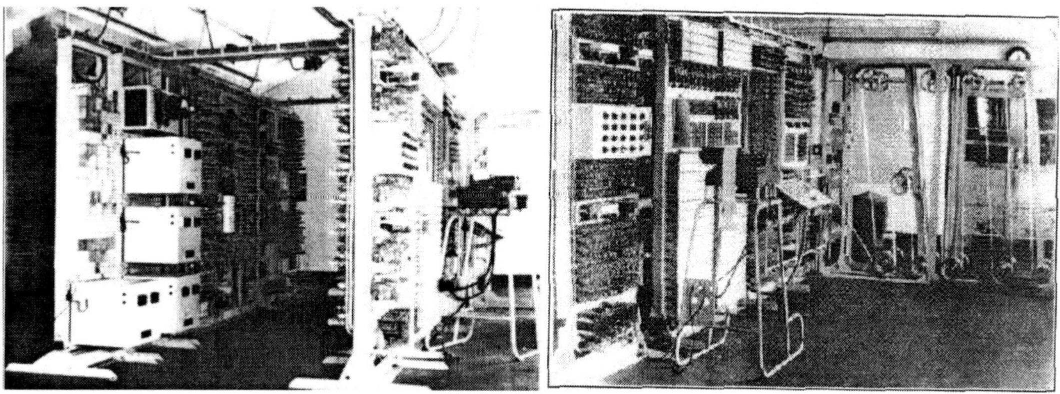

Figure 8.1 Two Views of a MK II Colossus
(The National Archives, London)

Neither these photographs, nor contemporary documents, indicate that Colossus was outfitted with a paper tape punch.[1] However, we must assume that Colossus had the ability to punch paper tapes since paper tape was the medium of data transfer between the various machines.*

---

* Paper tape punches were also called "perforators" at GCHQ

Colossus Design

There were two versions of Colossus, MK I and MK II. Colossus MK I has been described as experimental. This machine, only one of which was built, was a transition machine between the Robinsons and the Colossus MK II. Figure 8.2 shows the time line for the development, construction and deployment of the Colossi. Note the short time between the start of the design of Robinson and Colossus MK I. This indicates that the limitations of Robinson were apparent shortly after its design began. Note that Colossus MK II design was not started for ten months. The delay was probably caused by a shortage of design engineers and a desire to see how Flowers' ideas would work out in practice.

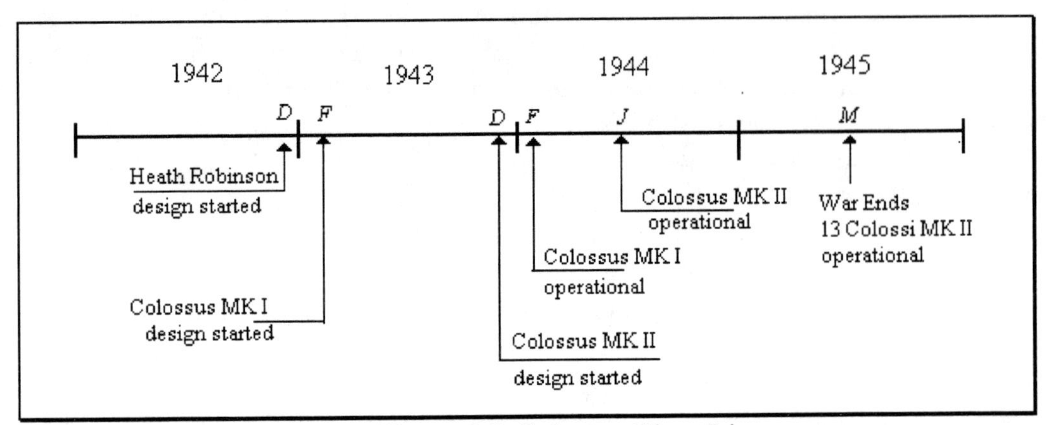

Figure 8.2 Colossus Time Line

Flowers' solution to the tape synchronization and wear problems and changes to increase the performance over the Robinson had four components.

1. Replace the keytext tape with an electronic keytext generator. Only one active bedstead would be required for the ciphertext tape.
2. Speedup the ciphertext tape to 5,000 characters per second.
3. Drive the single tape with rollers and sense the sprocket hole to provide clock pulses to the balance of the system. This eliminated sprocket hole tearing and made all of the logic of the machine synchronous from a common clock.
3. Increase the processing power by performing five double deltas at once.
4. Replace the Robinson phase logic scheme with a voltage level scheme.

Tommy Flowers' approach to the Colossus design required the use of a large number of vacuum tubes; 1,500 in the first Colossus grew to 2,400 in the last one produced. There was little faith that the large number of vacuum tubes needed would operate for even a short time without failure. A heavy bomber of the day had less than 100 tubes and they were always failing.* Flowers had to make a hard sell to be permitted to design an electronic device with 1,500 vacuum tubes.

* Coombs reports that "A colleague once said to me 'Valves? Don't like them. Nasty things. They Break.' This attitude lead to the phase shift logic of Robinson that reduced the number of tubes. As most tubes of the day were used in linear amplifiers, few designers and users had experience with tubes in applied in a

Nevertheless, Flowers prevailed and convinced the skeptics at Bletchley Park that a machine using vacuum tubes could be built that would be more reliable and faster than Robinson. A decision was made in February 1943 to start the design and construction of the Colossus MK I. The total speed increase over Robinson would be 2.5 due to the increase in tape speed.* [2] It was believed, correctly, that additional speed would have a lower total cost than additional slower speed machines.

Figure 8.3 is a block diagram of Colossus. The major features illustrated here are the use of an "Electronic Keytext Generator" in place of the Robinson keytext tape. There is only one bedstead and a printer for recording logical relationships. The "Logic" block could be patched to perform a number of algorithms such as double delta and rectangling.

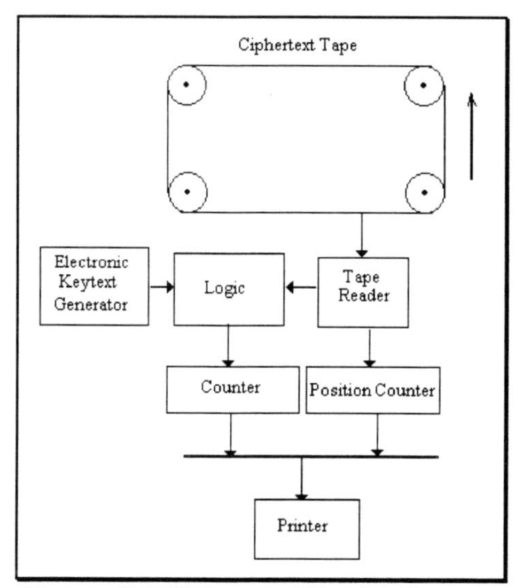

Figure 8.3 Colossus Block Diagram

Additional details of the connections between the Electronic Keytext Generators (called "thyratron ring stores), tape reader, shift register stores, 4 decade counters, and the printer are shown in Figure 8.4.

switching mode, with the power always on, and in a well-controlled environment. This was the Colossus environment, not use and environment in a heavy bomber that the critics were familiar with..

* Colossus MK II had an additional speed increase of 5X by the use of five-fold parallelism. The speedup of Colossus MK II over Robinson was, therefore, 12.5.

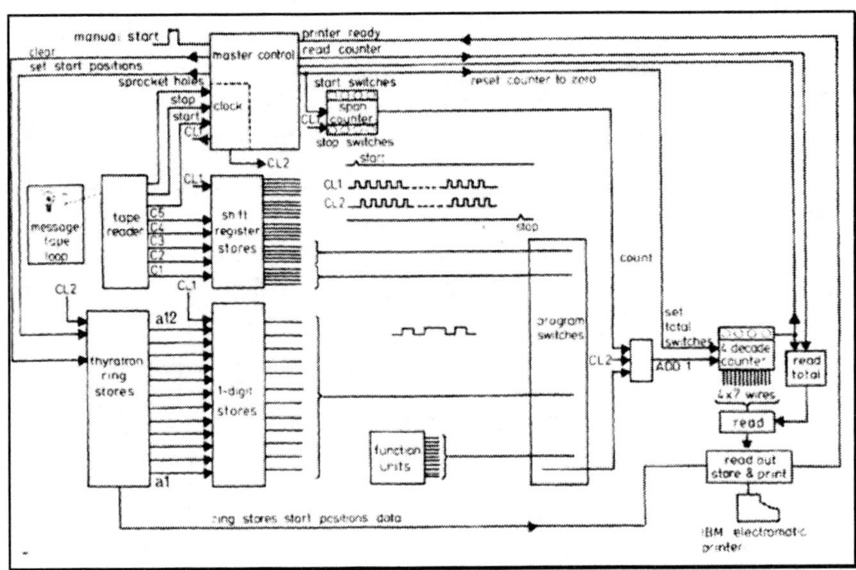

Figure 8.4 Colossus Block Diagram
(© 1983 IEEE)

Unfortunately this figure does not show the mod2 adders, which were the heart of the double delta algorithm. The reason for this omission can only be a guess. It is likely that Flowers believed in 1983 that this algorithm was still classified and should not be divulged. And it turns out that the algorithm was not disclosed until the 1990s. Although Flowers did not disclose the algorithm in 1983, he did provide hints in his description of the mod2 adder circuit. Also shown in this figure is a component called the "thyratron ring stores" that is the Electronic Keytext Generator of Figure 8.3.

The thyratron ring stores or Electronic Keytext Generators were electronic analogues of the Lorenz wheels, described later in this chapter.* The Electronic Keytext Generator produced strings of ones and zeros electronically rather than by reading a keytext tape as with Robinson.

A major system design consideration for Colossus was flexibility. It was known that a large group of algorithms would be most effective for wheel setting and other tasks. In this era before store-programmed computers, patching or wiring together the components provided the needed flexibility. Thus new algorithms could be wired, tested, and used. Figure 8.4 implies significant hard wiring between the major blocks, such as the tape reader, shift registers, the thyratron ring stores, and the 1-digit stores. These connections were not hard wired in Colossus; the connections were quite flexible as they were made by switches, relays, and patch cables.[3]

Telephone engineers working on the design of Colossus naturally chose to use standard two-wire cables, plugs, and sockets. The success of this system design philosophy was found in the large number of algorithms that could be executed. As the various components of Colossus are described, note will be made of the patching features.

* The Electronic Keytext Generator is an early programmable-read-only-memory or PROM.

Systolic Array Processor

The block labeled "Logic" in Figure 8.3, and not identified in Figure 8.4, can be plugged up as a systolic array, which performs five double deltas in parallel. This is the first use, known to the author, of a systolic array. [4]

The use of a systolic array is illustrated by further examining the example found in Chapter 7, *Wheel Setting on Old Robinson,* a ciphertext of 12 characters and a keytext of four characters. Although Colossus could process five double deltas in parallel, a systolic array of only four stages will be used here to illustrate the principle used in Colossus.

With a systolic array of four operation stages, the required number of steps will be reduced to approximately 1/4 the number of steps required by Robinson. Figure 8.5 shows a block diagram of a highly abstracted four stage systolic array. The ciphertext character stream, Z, enters one character at time from the ciphertext tape.

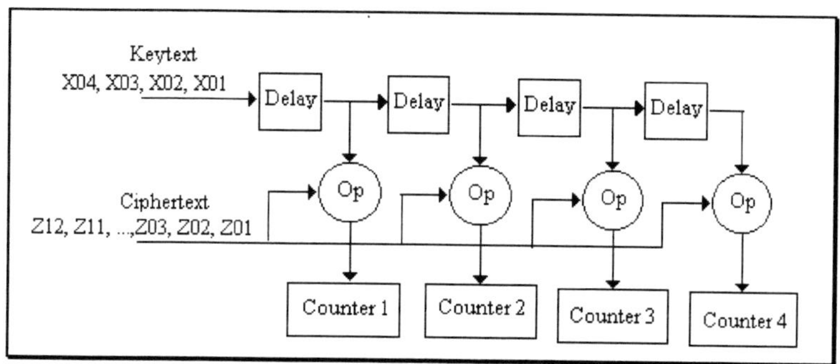

Figure 8.5, Four Stage Character Systolic Array

The ciphertext characters also enter one character at a time and are shifted down a shift register. Four keytext characters are present at any time. The keytext characters and a ciphertext character are processed in parallel in the four blocks called (Op) of the figure. Op is the kernel of the double delta algorithm.

The flows of the ciphertext and keytext streams, for the example in Chapter 7, are shown for the systolic array of Figure 8.5.

Step 1	X01 op Z01	—	—	—
Step 2	X02 op Z02	X01 op Z02	—	—
Step 3	X03 op Z03	X02 op Z03	X01 op Z03	—
Step 4	X04 op Z04	X03 op Z04	X02 op Z04	X01 op Z04
Step 5	**X01 op Z05**	**X04 op Z05**	**X03 op Z05**	**X02 op Z05**
Step 6	X02 op Z06	X01 op Z06	X04 op Z06	X03 op Z06
Step 7	X03 op Z07	X02 op Z07	X01 op Z07	X04 op Z07
Step 8	X04 op Z08	X03 op Z08	X02 op Z08	X0` op Z08
Step 9	X01 op Z09	X04 op Z09	X03 op Z09	X02 op Z09
Step 10	X02 op Z10	X 01op Z10	X04 op Z10	X03 op Z10
Step 11	X03 op Z11	X02 op Z11	X01 op Z11	X04 op Z11
Step 12	X04 op Z12	X03 op Z12	X02 op Z12	X01 op Z12
Step 13	—	X04 op Z01	X03 op Z01	X02 op Z01
Step 14	—	—	X04 op Z02	X03 op Z02
Step 15	—	—	—	X04 op Z03

At Step 1, X01 op Z01 is performed. At Step 2, X02 op Z02 and X02 op Z01 are performed. At Step 4, all of the Op stages are active and four operations are being performed at one time. Notice that at Step 5, for example, he ciphertext character Z05 is being processed with four keytext characters, X01, X04, X03, and, X02. The keytext characters are recycled as they pass through the shift register.

The four counters shown in Figure 8.5 count the zero tokens of the columns, above, to form the four scores needed for this example. Fifteen steps are required to perform the X_1 and X_2 wheel setting. As noted in Chapter 7, the same operation required 48 time steps on Robinson with only one Op stage and one counter. The reduction in the number of steps would be greater (and would approach the theoretical reduction of 4) with longer ciphertext and keytext streams, which reduce the impact of the pipeline start up and flush time.

A block diagram of the Colossus systolic array, patched for the Double Delta Algorithm, is shown in Figure 8.6. For the Colossus design, five stages of shift register were employed giving a five-fold speed improvement.

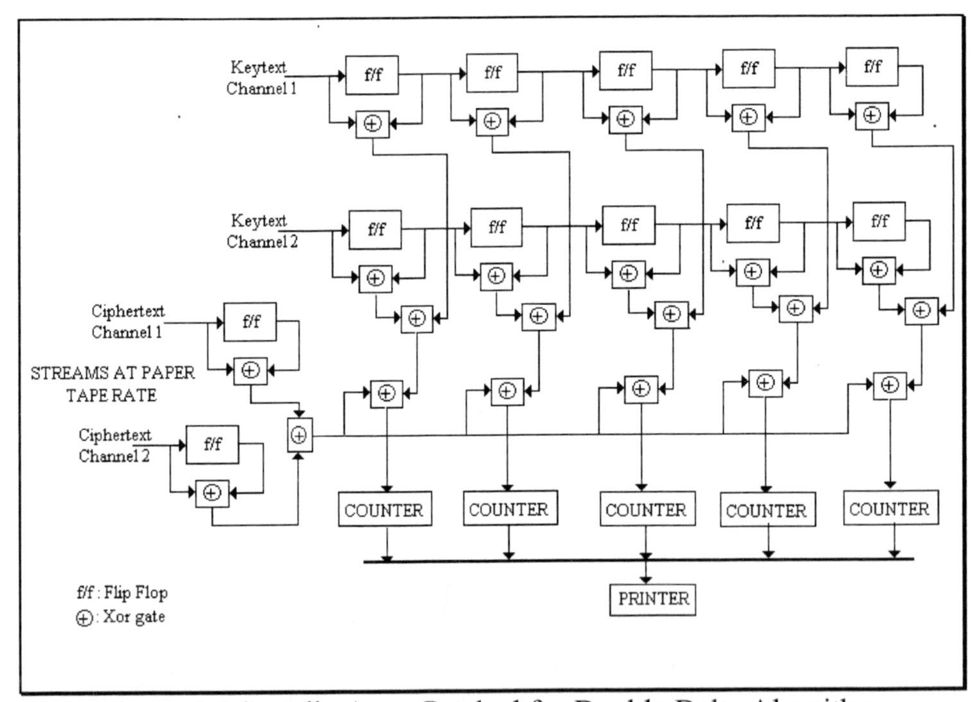

Figure 8.6 Systolic Array Patched for Double Delta Algorithm

The shift register stages are implemented with vacuum tubes (seven tubes per stage) as were the Xor gates (four tubes per gate) as described by Flowers.[5 6] The keytext character streams were implemented in thyratron shift registers that sequenced a plug programmable capacitor matrix. Several sets of the plug programmable capacitor matrixes were provided so that one wheel setting run could be set up as another wheel setting run was in progress.

The ciphertext character stream comes from the punched paper tape bedstead at 5,000 characters per second. Likewise, the keytext characters arrive from the Electronic Keytext Generator also at 5,000 characters of two bits per second. Thus a new ciphertext character is introduced into the array every 200 microseconds. After the Electronic Keytext Generator fills the shift register, five tokens are counted in the five counters on every cycle or input ciphertext character.* For a ciphertext message of 20,000 characters, five scores are printed every four seconds.

The Colossus systolic array provided for simultaneous processing of all five channels of the ciphertext and keytext streams, not just two channels as shown in Figure 8.6 Thus in one interval of 200 microseconds, the parity of five groups of 20 bits could be computed. This performance could not have been achieved with the technology of the day without the innovation of the systolic array.

The time to perform wheel setting on Colossus with parallelism of five is:

$$\text{Time} \approx (\text{Length of } X \times \text{Length of } Z) \div (\text{Tape character rate} \times \text{No. Stages in array})$$
$$\approx (\text{Length of } X \times \text{Length of } Z) \div (\text{Tape character rate} \times 5).$$

This processing time model is identical to that of the Robinson except for the number of stages in the array. The tape speed of Colossus was 5,000 characters per second. For Colossus MK II, wheel setting of Channels 1 and 2 and a 10,000-character ciphertext message, wheel setting would take 8.5 minutes, a speedup of 12.5X over Robinson. Albert Small writes that the time was approximately 8 minutes.[7]

Colossus Ciphertext Tape Format

The ciphertext tape format is almost identical to that used with Robinson and is shown in Figure 8. 7.

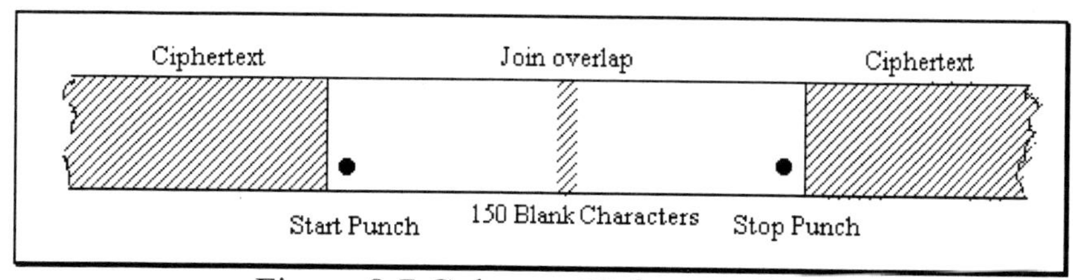

Figure 8.7 Colossus Ciphertext Tape

The major difference in this format from the Robinson format is the reduction in the number of blank characters from 2,000 to 150. One reason for this reduction is that with more electronics and fewer relays, the time needed to synchronize from one pass to the next can be reduced.

Wheel Breaking with Colossus

The original design goal for Robinson and Colossus was to perform wheel setting. Wheel breaking was to be a manual process performed in the Testery based on linguist insight and cryptographic skills. However, the desire to mechanize at least a part of wheel breaking was always present. This need became urgent when the Germans started changing the *X* and *S* pin patterns on a daily basis in July 1944.

In December 1942 Max Newman was given the assignment of developing machine methods for setting Fish ciphertext. This work resulted in the design of

* Figure 8.5 shows four counters, not five. Five are required to achieve five fold parallelism.

Robinson and Colossus. We can also assume that the work continued into techniques for wheel breaking. It cannot be known at this time who extended Tutte's work on rectangling into the design of the rectangling gadget described in the following paragraphs. However, the evidence indicates that research started before December 1943, about the same time that Colossus MK II design started. These dates suggest the wheel breaking was integral to the Colossus MK II concept.

Colossus Rectangling

The strategy for rectangling is to form the surplus-deficit count rectangle shown in Figure 5.2. This operation is labor intensive if done by hand and prone to error, thus the need for a mechanical aid. After the rectangle is formed, the assumed values of ΔX_1, ΔX_2, X_1, and $X2$ can be found by integration as discussed in Chapter 5.

There seems to have been an evolution in thinking about how to generate rectangles with the Colossus. The first, and most basic, approach was to stream the ciphertext tape and control the printer so that the $Z\oplus$s can be printed. This task was unsuited to Colossus and a special machine, called Garbo, was implemented to do this fundamental work of rectangling. Garbo is described in Chapter 10.

Donald Michie had the idea for using Colossus to support rectangling.[8] He showed how the logic elements of a Colossus could be interconnected to form the surplus-deficit count. An attachment or "gadget" was also devised for Colossus to assist in rectangling and print out the results. It is reasonable to assume that the insight gained with Garbo influenced the design of the gadget.

The basic idea of rectangling on Colossus was to scan the $Z\oplus$ stream in such a way that the selected elements are routed into each of the five counters. These counters will contain the count of the $Z\oplus$s =1 that will be eventually posted into the surplus-deficit rectangle. Thus what was needed was a scanning mechanism and routing paths that would send the selected values of $Z\oplus$ to the correct counter.

The example of Chapter 5, Figure 5.4, of a ciphertext of 60 characters and a keytext created by an X_1 wheel of three bits and an X_2 wheel of five bits will be used to illustrate this process as carried out on Colossus. Table 8.1 shows the stacking on the 3×5 rectangle. The character-numbers of the $Z\oplus$s are posted to the array starting with 1, then 2, 3, 4, and 5. This process repeats until all 60 $Z\oplus$s have been posted.

Table 8.1 Stacking in Depth

	$X_{2,1}$	$X_{2,2}$	$X_{2,3}$	$X_{2,4}$	$X_{2,5}$
$X_{1,1}$	1 16 31 46	7 22 37 52	13 28 43 58	4 19 34 49	10 25 40 55
$X_{1,2}$	11 26 41 56	2 17 32 47	8 23 38 53	14 29 44 59	5 20 35 50
$Z_{1,3}$	6 21 36 51	12 27 42 57	3 18 33 48	9 24 39 54	15 30 45 60

Figure 8.8 shows patching of Colossus to rectangle this example. Note that a sequence 1, 7, 13, 4, 10 must be extracted and routed to the five counters. One of the two shift registers is patched with five stages and with feedback.* The other shift register is

* These shift registers are only one bit wide as compared to the available 5 bit width when all five bits of a Baudot code are shifted.

patched into a three stage register with feedback. The five stage register is loaded with a single one and four zeros. The three stage register is loaded with a single one and two zeros.

The four counters count the Z⊕s in the shaded intersections of Table 8.1 on the first pass. The other intersections are counted on following passes.

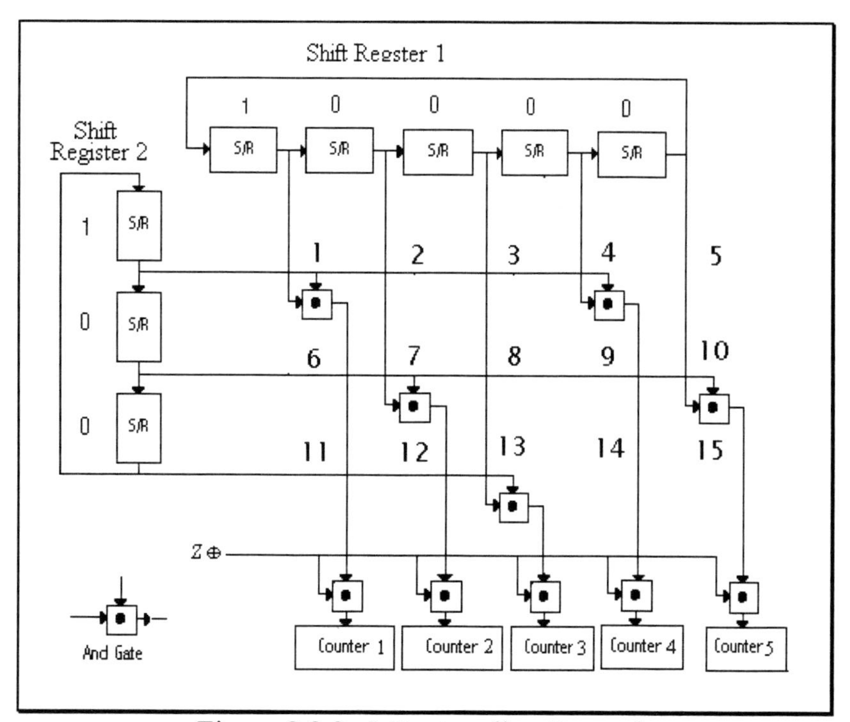

Figure 8.8 3×5 Rectangling Example

The 1 in the five stage shift register, called SR 1, is shifted to the right. After four shifts, the 1 is shifted around to the input of SR 1 and SR 2 shifts one place. In this way, the array is scanned. By this scanning, the intersections of the array are enabled in the sequence 1, 2, 3,...,15. However, only the intersections with AND gates send the *Z*⊕s to one of the five counters. Therefore, the *Z*⊕s of the addresses 1, 4, 7, 10, and 13 are counted. On subsequent passes, the other *Z*⊕s are routed to the counters.

Table 8.2Rectangling, First Pass

Step	SR1	SR2	Ctr. 1	Ctr. 2	Ctr. 3	Ctr. 4	Ctr. 5
1	10000	100	1				
2	01000	100					
3	00100	100					
4	00010	100				4	
5	00001	100					
6	10000	010					
7	01000	010		7			
8	00100	010					
9	00010	010					
10	00001	010					10
11	10000	001					
12	01000	001					
13	00100	001			13		
14	00010	001					
15	00001	001					

After all of the passes (four for this example), Counter 1 has counted the $Z\oplus$s, 1, 16, 31, and 46. Counter 2 has counted the, 7, 22, 37, and 52. Counter 3 has counted the $Z\oplus$s 13, 28, 43 and 58. And so on. These counts are exactly the counts called for in Table 8.1.

After these results of five cells are printed, two more cycles of four passes of the ciphertext tape are required to complete all fifteen cells of the rectangle. Note that when the counters are printed out, the results are a row of the rectangle.

The output is a printed rectangle with a count of the $Z\oplus$s in each of the intersections. From this, the Surplus-deficit values (Figure 5.2) can be computed by hand.

Figure 8.9 shows the shift registers, logic and counters used with Colossus patched for the rectangling portion of wheel breaking. The special keytext streams representing Channels 1 and 2 are introduced into the two shift registers. The Channel 1 shift register is shifted on each clock while the Channel 2 shift register is under the control of the Channel 1 shift register.

Two channels of the ciphertext Z are streamed into the system at the lower left, the flip flops and gates produce the stream of $Z\oplus$ signals. The desired $Z\oplus$s are grabbed by the row of AND gates at the bottom of the figure and routed to the proper counter.

The special keytext pattern introduced into both the shift registers consists of a single one and 40 or 30 bits of zero. As with Figure 8.8, the single one in the Channel 1 shift register enables the column lines in sequence. With a single one in the first stage of the Special Keytext Channel 2 shift register, the first intersection of the array is scanned.

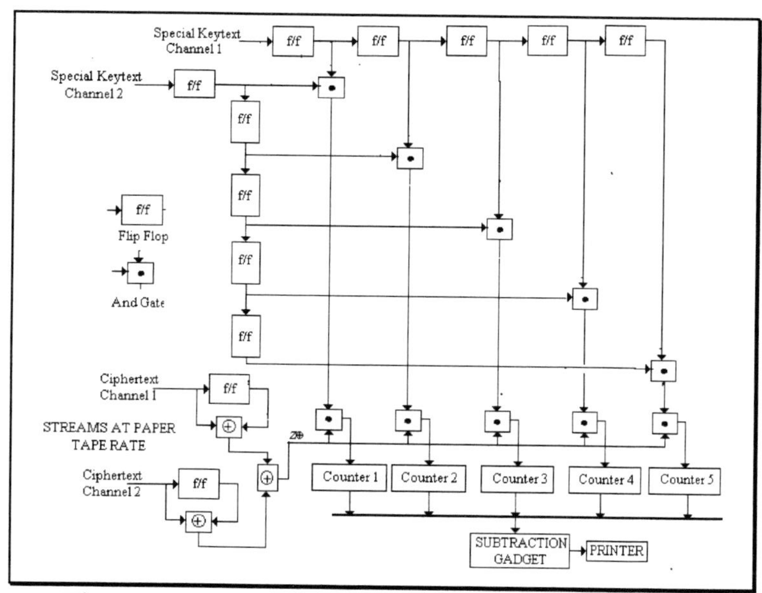

Figure 8.9, Systolic Array Patched For Rectangling

Note that there was no feedback on the shift registers as in Figure 8.8 as the special triggers produce continuous streams of the patterns and the feedback was incorporated in their design.

The special keytext generator for X_1 had 40 zeros and 1 one. The X_2 keytext generator had 30 zeros and 1 one. However, unlike wheel setting runs which stepped all keytext generators together, these two keytext generators do not run in synchrony. X_2 can be selected by a switch to step at the clock rate. Then each time the last stage of *X2* has a one, it will step *X1*.

Assume that the initial conditions of both X_1 and X_2 wheel generators are 1. The coincidence of these two keytext generators will select the 1,1 cell of the rectangle. As X_2 steps, cell 1,2 then cell 1,3 and so on will be selected. As these points are scanned, the AND gates at each intersection is routed to another AND gate, the output is combined with the Z⊕ signal and sent to a counter. Flowers shows the circuit for an AND gate which he calls "Boolean addition."[9]

To obtain the surplus-deficit count for each intersection of the rectangle could require two runs on the tape. One run would be needed to count the zero Z⊕ and a second run to count the one Z⊕s. The approach taken with Colossus, however, was to make one run, count only the one Z⊕s and compute the surplus-deficit. The surplus-deficit is found by arithmetically doubling the count of the Z⊕s and adding the depth.[*] [10]

The Subtraction Gadget performed this function after the operator set the depth on switches, 1-32. The implementation of this gadget is believed to be by relay lookup tables and is being reverse engineered for the Colossus replica project.[11]

[*] #0s + # 1s = depth. #0s = depth – #1s. Thus Surplus-deficit = #0s – #1s = (depth – # 1s) - #1s = depth - 2*#1s.

Rectangling Setup Panel

In addition to the special patching of the shift register elements and logic, a method was provided to supply the Special Ciphertext Channels X_1 and X_2 patterns. These patterns were provided by a special control panel and thyratron shift registers.

Figure 8.10 is a photograph of the special trigger panel on the front of Colossus. By means of the plugs shown in this photograph, keytext patterns could be set up for use in regular wheel setting. There were two pluggable patterns and one fixed pattern.

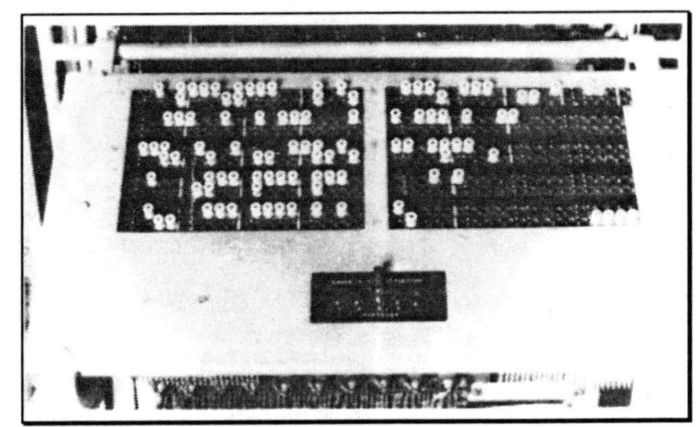

Figure 8.10 Rectangling Setup Panel, Special Triggers
(The National Archives, London)

The two pluggable patterns were called ordinary X trigger and special X trigger patterns. A third pattern, which was not pluggable, had a single 1 in the last positions of X_1 and X_2, the patterns used in the shift registers needed for rectangling.

Five three-way switches (one for each of the X wheels) in the foreground control the 5 X wheel patterns.[12] The switch positions were:

1. Down: ordinary and special patterns in
2. Normal: all out
3. Up: single cross in the last position of the ordinary pattern.

Another photograph of a Colossus is shown in Figure 8.11. This view clearly shows the rectangling control panel to the right of the operator on the left. This photograph also gives a good view of the serpentine path of a tape on a bedstead.

Figure 8.11 Colossus with Rectangling Setup Panel
(The National Archives, London)

Sequencing the Rectangle

Rectangling is unlike wheel setting. With wheel setting, key values are saved in the shift registers for use on a subsequent ciphertext character. With rectangling, there are no saved values so only one *Z*⊕ can be counted for each pass of the ciphertext tape, unless there is more than one counter. Thus, with five counters, on one pass of the ciphertext tape, five *Z*⊕s can be counted. On the next pass, five more will be counted and so on.

For a 12,710 character ciphertext, counter 1 will count the *Z*⊕s for cells 1, 1272, 2,543, 3,814, 5,085, 6,356, 7,627, 8,898, 10,169, and 11,440. * Only one *Z*⊕ is added to any one counter on each pass. However, counter 2 is counting *Z*⊕ 2, 1273, 2544, and so on. With five counters, the number of passes over the ciphertext required to compute a rectangle is reduced by a factor of 5 compared to the number of passes required on Robinson with only one counter.

There was a problem because the dimensions of the rectangle are 41×31 and 5 is not a factor of either dimension as 41 and 31 are prime with no factors. The available literature does not specifically address how the rectangling was scheduled around this problem. Filling in 5 cells at a time on a rectangle of 40×30 will work as 5 is a factor of both 40 and 30. A more likely approach was to rectangle a 45×35 rectangle and accept that there will be redundancies.[13]

There are as many *Z*⊕s as characters in the ciphertext, consequently the number of passes is (Length of *Z*÷5). And, the time required for a pass is the (Length of *Z* ÷ 5,000). Thus the time required to rectangle is:

$$\text{Time} \approx (\text{Length of } Z \div 5) \times (\text{Length of } Z \div 5{,}000)$$
$$\approx (\text{Length of } Z)^2 \div 25{,}000 \text{ seconds.}$$

* Actually Colossus differenced and rectangled from the end of the ciphertext tape, not the beginning as described above.

For a 12,710 character ciphertext, the time to rectangle is:

Time $\approx 12{,}710^2 \div 25{,}000 \approx 6{,}461$ second ≈ 1.8 hours.

Rectangling a ciphertext message on Robinson would require (Length of $Z)^2 \div$ 2,000 seconds. Thus, for the 12,710 character ciphertext message, the time would be 80,772 seconds or 22.4 hours. Clearly rectangling on Robinson was attempted only occasionally.

Finding the ΔXs and Xs

There is little evidence in the available documents to suggest that the Colossi did anything other than rectangling for wheel breaking. In most cases, the process of finding Δ*X*s and *X*s, from the surplus-deficit count, described in Chapter 4, must have been done by hand. However, a process called "converging" could be executed on Colossus, which performs some of the work of finding Δ*X*s and *X*s.[14] Evidently this process was used infrequently for special cases, as the hand method was more effective.

Spanning

Frequently, ciphertext tapes were received with stretches of garbled information. This garbled stretch could not be processed as it would corrupt the statistical basis for both wheel setting and wheel breaking.

Thus a feature incorporated in Colossus MK II was called "spanning." This feature permitted the specification of a span of ciphertext to be processed that was a portion of the total ciphertext. Near the top-center of Figure 8.4 will be seen start switches and stop switches. These switches specified the span over which the processing is active.

Spanning was not incorporated in Robinson. However, spanning was found to have great utility with the Colossi.

Circuits

As noted earlier, the major improvements in speed and reliability of Colossus over Robinson resulted from Tommy Flowers' decision to adopt vacuum tube circuits on a grand scale. The circuits described below have a very modern appearance for that pre-transistor age. Even with the multi-million gate devices of today, the basic circuit ideas are still apparent. The following sections describe these circuits and the changes to the bedstead design.

Design Standards

To accomplish the four improvements over Robinson noted earlier Flowers made a foresighted decision. Most electronic circuits adopted for Colossus Mark II would be electrically modular and standard throughout the machine. This is a practice that was not adopted by the computer industry until the 1950s.[15] These standards were:[16]

1. All logic signals would be DC voltages carried by a pair of wires, now known as two-rail logic. Each wire carried the complement of the other wire, a design

that fitted well with the use of standard telephone cables, plugs and jacks. The DC logic values were less than -35 volts and slightly higher than zero or ground as shown in Figure 8.12.

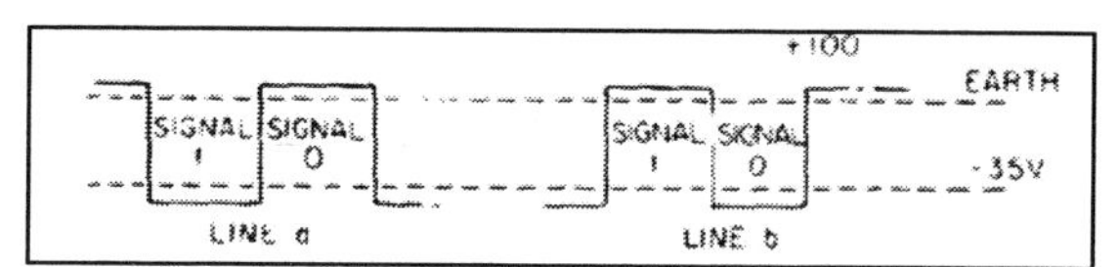

Figure 8.12 Standard Logic Levels
(© 1983 IEEE)

2. All logic signals were transmitted to other circuits via a standard output buffer shown in Figure 8.13. The load driving of this output buffer is not clear from the literature: one load, two loads, three loads?

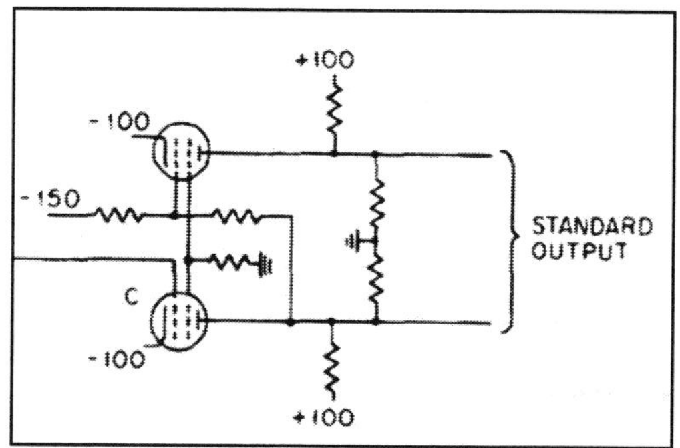

Figure 8.13 Standard Output Buffer
(© 1983 IEEE)

3. Other standards were set for the selection of vacuum tubes, high voltage values, and the distribution of filament voltages.

We have seen in Chapter 7 that Robinson was cobbled together to get something working.* On the other hand, the Colossus Mark II was carefully engineered and only the circuits and techniques that had proved to be functional and reliable on Robinson were carried forward. Revolutionary computer-type design and construction techniques were developed and employed.

Electronic Keytext Generator

As we have seen, an electronic keytext generator replaced the keytext tape of Robinson. Pulse streams were needed having the same length as the twelve wheels (41, 31, 29, 26, 23, 43, 47, 51, 53, 59, 61, and 37) of the Lorenz. The electronic keytext generators were called “triggers” at BP.†

The keytext generator portion of Colossus was in effect an electronic version of the Lorenz machine itself. Because of this, Colossus was used to decipher messages after wheel breaking and wheel setting had been completed. This flexibility of Colossus eliminated the need for newer, higher speed versions of Tunny.

---

* Today the Robinsons might be called “breadboard” systems.

† Small, pg. 108, used the term trigger to indicate a stepping switch.

The electronic keytext generator consisted of 12 shift registers, which produced pulses with the same patterns as the pins of the 12 wheels of the Lorenz (the a1 to a12 of the thyratron ring store of Figure 8.4). Each of the 12 outputs is buffered with a standard output buffer. These registers were implemented using thyratrons as shown in Figure 8.14. Thyratron ring counters had proved to be reliable for Robinson token counting and were redesigned for the electronic keytext generators in Colossus.

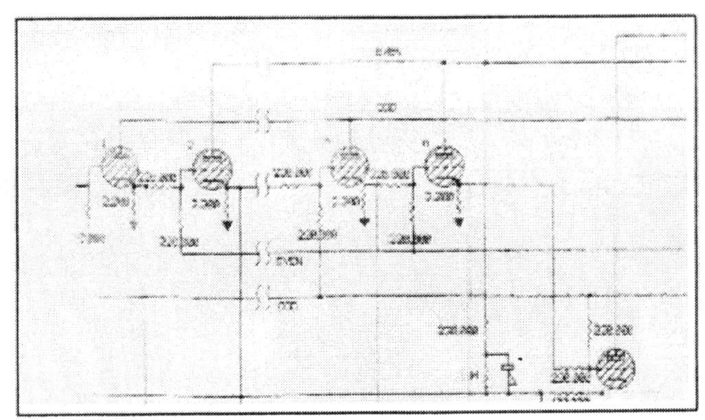

Figure 8.14 Thyratron Ring[17]
(Courtesy of Tony Sale)

A thyratron is a gas-filled triode tube, which is commonly used as a rectifier. The grid controls conduction between the cathode and anode. Conduction, once initiated, must be extinguished to place the thyratron into the non-conducting state. Thus a thyratron can act as a one bit memory or store. Each ring has as many thyratrons as pins on a Lorenz wheel, 42, 31, etc for a total of 501 ring positions.

The thyratron ring circuits were designed by Tommy Flowers, not carried forward from the Wynn-Williams' design of the Robinson counters.[18] The ring of thyratrons would shift a single "one" around in a circle. The anodes of alternate thyratrons were energized and the "one" state of a conducting thyratron was shifted one place to the right with each synchronizing pulse from the keytext tape sprocket hole. Because eleven of the twelve wheels have an odd number of pins, special circuits were needed to make the ring appear to be of even length so that the anodes could be grouped in pairs.

Figure 8.15 shows the thyratron ring for generating X_1 pulses which mimic the output of the X_1 wheel of a Lorenz. A wheel pattern was set by switching in resistors with standard telephone shorting plugs from the 41-position thyratron ring. Inserting a shorting plug would close the switch, generating a "one." An omitted shorting plug would generate a "zero." The thyratron output transitions were coupled into a staticisor*, with a suitable change to the input circuit, to give a stream of ones and zeros.

* A staticisor is a circuit that converts an analogue signal into a digital signal of "ones" and "zeros."

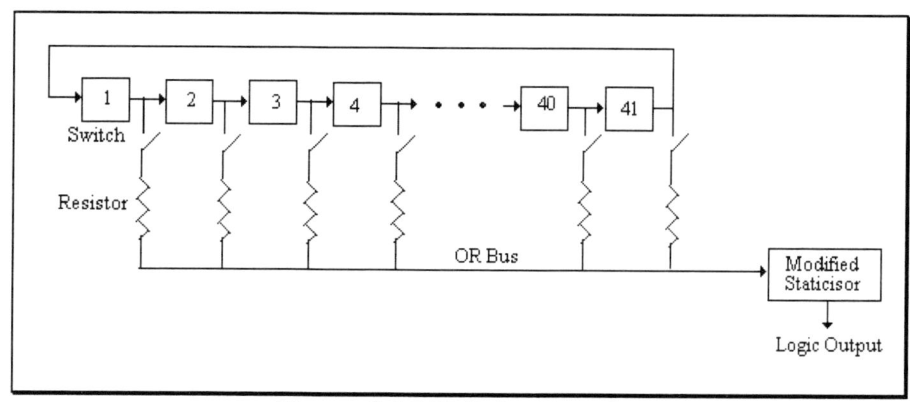

Figure 8.15 X_1 Pulse Forming

Figure 8.16 shows the switch bank for the X_2 thyratron ring located on the back of the front right frame shown in Figure 8.1. It is reported that this location of the plugs was inconvenient for the operators.[19]

Figure 8.16 X_2 Wheel Thyratron Switch Bank
(The National Archives, London)

A U-shaped pin (shorting plug) was inserted into the plugs of the switch bank to couple a one onto the OR bus. The absence of a pin gave a zero. Wheels for the X and S patterns can be selected from five alternative pin patterns (A, B, C, D, and E); the Motor wheels M_1 and M_2 had seven alternative selections. One set of pin patterns was programmed and reserved for testing. A standard ciphertext tape with reserved patterns would be run to verify the proper operation of the Colossus. Although not a thorough test, it gave a qualitative indication of the health of the machine.

Speedup the Ciphertext Tape to 5,000 Characters per second.

Recall from Chapter 7 that Robinson used two paper tapes, one keytext and one ciphertext tape. The two tapes were driven from sprockets mounted on a common shaft. Due to stretching and tear on the sprocket holes and the distance between the sprocket and the mask, erratic results were frequent. With the decision to replace the keytext tape with an electronic keytext generator to overcome this problem it became possible to increase the tape speed. *

With only one tape, the decision was made to do away with the sprocket drive and drive the tape by a set of friction wheels. Because the sprocket hole would be sensed by the optical system generating a master clock pulse, small variations in the speed of the tape did not cause a timing problem.

Photocell Amplifier or Staticisor

Figure 8.17 shows the circuit that converted the outputs from the photocell amplifiers into standard digital voltage level outputs. Note that this amplifier was DC coupled, unlike the Robinson amplifier, and should not have given problems with strings of dots and crosses. As with the other output circuits, one of the output lines provided the true and the other output line the complement of the photocell output. There were 8 of these amplifiers, five for the five channels,† one for the sprocket hole, and two used to detect the special start and stop codes on the paper tape.

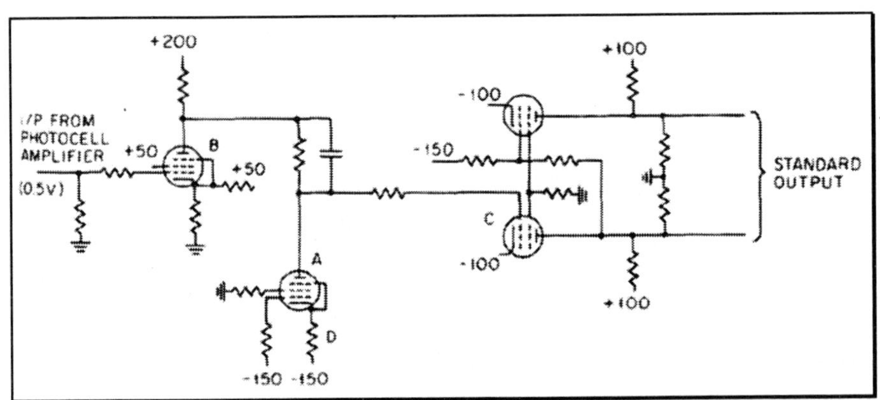

Figure 8.17 Photocell Output Amplifier or Staticisor
(© 1983 IEEE)

Shift Registers

Figure 8.18 shows the circuit for a single shift register stage. The input, A, to the stage was two-rail logic which could be patched from various sources. Likewise the output, C, could be patched to various destinations.

The sprocket hole pulse from the paper tape reader was differentiated by an RC network, amplified and used as the clock pulse. The true and complement A inputs were gated into a pair of buffers and sent to a flip-flop, which provided one bit of memory. The output buffers produced the true and complement pair at C. The operation of this shift register bit is similar to a modern RS flip flop.

---

* Tommy Flowers drove the tape at ever increasing speed until, at 9,000 characters per second, the tape broke. Flower notes that a major accomplishment of W.W.II was to demonstrate that paper tape could be driven at 60 miles per hour!

† Unlike Robinson that reads two characters at a time to form the double delta, Colossus used flip flop delays and needed to read only one character at a time.

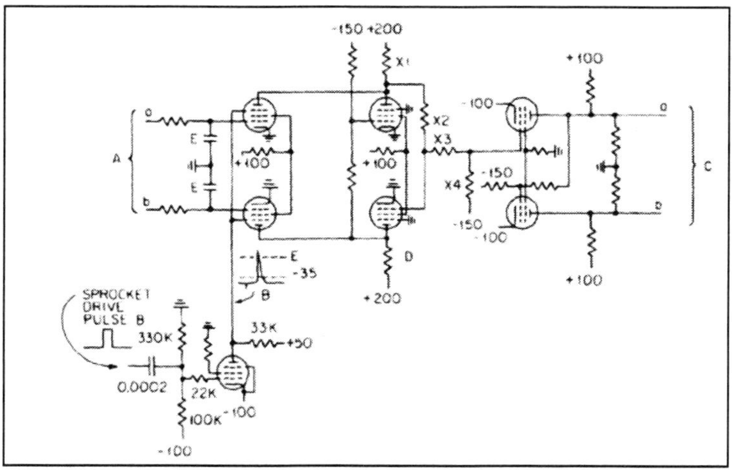

Figure 8.18 Shift Register Stage
(© 1983 IEEE)

The Colossus logic system is the first digital system, known to the author, which operated in a synchronous mode. That is, a central clock source was distributed to all of the flip flops that responded together to their inputs. Whereas the Colossus implementation was not as general as that found in computers a decade later, it likely was the first synchronous clocking system.

Cascading five of these stages provided a five-stage shift register.* The buffering would ensure that logic signals were propagated from stage to stage without loss or unwanted parasitic signals. As each stage of the shift register required 7 vacuum tubes, the total number of tubes for this function, for all five channels was 245 (7 × 5 × 7).

Xor Circuits

A vacuum tube Xor circuit was designed for Colossus, shown in Figure 8.19, to replace the phase logic of the Robinson. The true and complement signals for two inputs A and B were added together, mod2, in the two left-hand pentodes. The output of the addition (A ⊕ B = C) was placed in standard logic level form by the output buffer on the right of the figure.

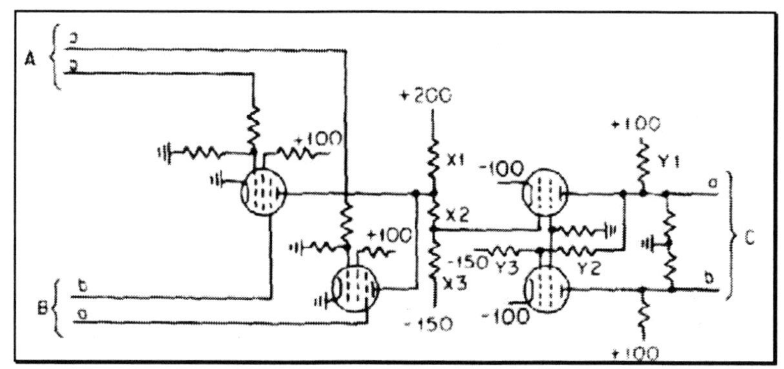

Figure 8.19 Colossus Xor Circuit
(© 1983 IEEE)

* It is not known if a clock driver amplifier was needed for each shift register stage.

Each "2-bit slice" of the systolic array, Figure 8.6, used 23 of these circuits. Thus, with four tubes per circuit, 92 tubes were required. Two hundred and thirty tubes were needed for the five deep systolic array.

Decade Counters

Decade counters, shown in Figure 8.20, count the outputs of the logic section of Colossus.* Because of the increased tape speed, the counters of the Robinson were inadequate. Thus all four stages of the counters were electronic decade counters based on a pre-war design by C. E. Wynn-Williams. Each decade counter consisted of a divide-by-two flip-flop[20] (probably the same circuit as Figure 8.18) followed by a five-stage shift register consisting of seven vacuum tubes.

Each of the five stages of the systolic array had five decade counters to count from 0 to 9,999. Thus, twenty-decade counters were required, each having 11 vacuum tubes (4 for the flip flop and 8 for the divide by five), for a total of 220 tubes. Another counter was required to count and record the electronic keytext generator position to count the sprocket pulses to record the wheel setting position. This required another 44 tubes for a total of 264 tubes.

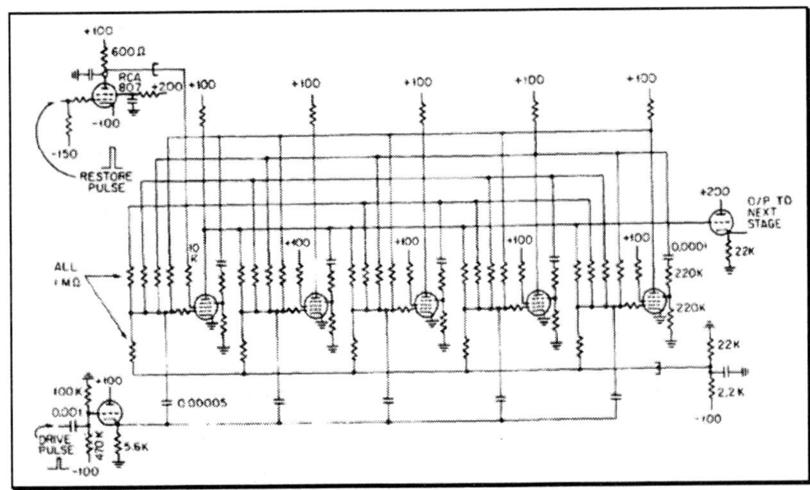

Figure 8.20 Scale-of-Five Counter

(© 1983 IEEE)

Printer

The counters accumulated the logical events to form the scores, which were then buffered into relay registers to await printing.† What printing rate would this process produce? When performing wheel settings, each cycle of the ciphertext tape would produce counts for the five wheel settings of the keytext. For a 10,000 character ciphertext tape, one print cycle would occur at 10000 / 5,000 = 2 seconds. At the end of this cycle, the printer was required to print 4 × 5 = 20 characters (four scores and the wheel setting of electronic the keytext generator). Thus the maximum required printing rate is 20 / 2 = 10 characters per second.

* These are the counters of Figures 8.3, 8.4, 8.5, 8.6, 8.8, and 8.9.

† To the author, this is a first known instance of buffering.

IBM Electromatic typewriters, Figure 8.21, were relatively common in the 1940s and were the printers used with Colossi.* [21] However, significant modifications were made to the typewriters by Tommy Flowers' engineers so that the typewriters would interface with a Colossus. The maximum printing rate of the IBM electric typewriters of the day was approximately 10 characters per second; performance was reduced with a carriage return.

Figure 8.21 IBM Electromatic Typewriter
(Courtesy of IBM Archives)

Consequently, this typewriter was marginally able to meet the required printing rate for wheel breaking ciphertext tapes of less than 10,000 characters. Shorter ciphertext tapes would require printing rates in excess of the Electromatic's ability. Longer ciphertext tapes, which have a lower printing rate requirement, could be accommodated.

Various steps were taken to overcome the printing rate problem for short ciphertext tapes. One step taken was to print only significant scores. Threshold values can be set in switches that inhibit printing of scores less than a given value. This feature can reduce the printing load by 30%-40% because, as discussed in Chapter 5, only scores large enough to be possible candidates for indicating a probable wheel settings need to be printed.

Another step taken was to print the eight characters without a space, to eliminate the need to provide a space that would slow the printing process. For example, 25431798 means position 2534 with a score of 1798. These IBM Electromatic typewriters printed at a reduced rate when two or more identical characters were to be printed. So arbitrary letters were substituted for all but the last identical character. For example, ab072f39 meant 00072339.

---

* IBM Electromatic typewriters were supplied under Lend-Lease to Britain during the war.

Hardware modifications, called a "Gadget", to the printer control were made to print in the output of a rectangling run. There were three modifications:[22]

1. The carriage return was operative only at the end of a row of the rectangle.
2. The X_1 and X_2 position settings were not printed.
3. Each score was printed as a single figure 0-9.

As the depth was known, scores greater than 9 could be computed; it was not necessary to print more than one character. However, the digits had to be signed requiring two printed figures, not one.

Concluding Observation

There are two versions of Colossus mentioned in the literature, MK I and MK II. The exact differences between these two are unclear from the evidence available today, although the MK I version did not incorporate the systolic array.[23] The speedup of Mark I over Robinson was due completely to the inclusion of electronic keytext generators along with the increase in paper tape speed, 5,000 characters per second compared to 2,000 characters per second. The increase in paper tape speed also required that all stages of the counters be electronic.

The Colossus MK II had two significant improvements over MK I. It incorporated the systolic array giving a five-fold speedup over MK I. It also had the attachment, described in Section 8.5.1 for performing rectangling.[24] It is not known if the special keytext generators shared the thyratron shift registers with the other keytext generators. If not shared, another 501 tubes would have been added to the Mark II tube count.

Another change is implied. The photo mask for reading the paper tape probably had only one row of apertures, not the two of Robinson. A character was read once and the delay was achieved by a shift register stage as shown in Figure 8.6. Flowers writes "using a tape reader that had to read only one line at a time and was thus simplified compared with the readers first used with the Robinson machines.[25] By having only one aperture, most of the sensitivity to the speed of the tape would be eliminated giving a more reliable system.

An estimate of the number of tubes used in each section of the Mark I and Mark II is given in Table 8.3.

Table 8.3 Estimate of Tube Count

Circuit	Mark I	Mark II
Electronic Keytext Generators	501	501
Photo Cell Amplifiers	52	64
Shift Register		245
Xor	28	240
Rectangle Gadget Keytext		501
Subtraction Gadget		100
Spanning Counter		96
Decade Counters.	28	264
Estimated Total	605	2,011
Reported Total	1,500	2,400

The estimated tube count is lower than the count reported in the references. Clearly all of the tube uses have not been identified.

On June 6, 1996, a replica of a Colossus built by Tony Sale was turned on at Bletchley Park. Figure 8.22 is a photograph of the event. From left to right are: Dr. Tommy Flowers, HRH the Duke of Kent, and Tony Sale.

Figure 8.22 Colossus Replica Turn-on
(Courtesy of Tony Sale)

This chapter on Colossus is concluded with a quotation from *General Report on Tunny*"[26]

> "It is regretted that it is not possible to give an adequate idea of the fascination of a Colossus at work: its sheer bulk and apparent complexity; the fantastic speed of thin paper tape round the glittering pulleys; the childish pleasure of not-not, span, print main heading and other gadgets; the wizardry of purely mechanical decoding letter by letter (one novice thought she was being hoaxed); the uncanny action of the typewriter in printing the correct scores without and beyond human aid; the stepping of display; periods of eager expectation culminating in the sudden appearancc of the longed-for score; the strange rhythms characterizing every type of run; the stately break-in, the erratic short run, the regularity of wheel-breaking, the stolid rectangle interrupted by the wild leaps of the carriage-return, the frantic chatter of a motor run, the ludicrous frenzy of hosts of bogus scores."

References

[1] Michie, D., Good, J., Timms, G., *General Report on Tunny*, 1945, Released to the Public Record Office in 2000, http://www.alanturing.net/tunny_report, pg. 326.
[2] Flowers, T., "The Design of Colossus," *The Annals of the History of Computing,* Vol. 5, No. 3, July 1983, pp. 239-252.
[3] E-mail communication from Tony Sale, 2002.
[4] Kung, H.T., "Why Systolic Architectures?," *Computer*, vol. 15, no. 1, January 1982, pp. 37-46
[5] (Flowers, The Design, 249).
[6] Sale, A.E., *The Colossus: its purpose and operations*, http://www.codesandciphers.org.uk/lorenz/colossus.htm.
[7] Small, A.W., *Special Fish Report,* NARA, NR. 4628, Box 1417, December 1944, pg. 111. Also available at: http://www.codesandciphers.org.uk/documents/smallix.htm. pg. 8.

---

[8] Good, J., "Enigma and Fish". *Codebreakers, The Inside Story of Bletchley Park,* Ed. Hinsley, F. H., Stripp, A., Oxford University Press, 1993, pg. 164.
[9] (Flowers, The Design, 247).
[10] Anonymous, *Report on British Attack on "FISH",* Communications Intelligence Technical Paper TS 47, Navy Department, Washington D.C., May 1945, NARA RG 457, Box 607, pg. 64.
[11] e-mail, Tony Sale 7/12/02.
[12] Ecckles, W.H., Jordan, F. W. "A Trigger Relay Utilizing Three-Electrode Thermionic Vacuum Tubes," *Radio Review,* Vol. 1, Dec. 1919, pg. 335.
[13] (Anonymous, *Report*,50).
[14] (ibid. 63).
[15] Wilkes, M. V., "The Best Way to Design an Automatic Calculating Machine," *Manchester University Computer Inaugural Conference,* Ferranti Ltd. London, 1951.
[16] Coombs, A.W., "The Making of Colossus," *The Annals of the History of Computing*, Vol. 5, Number 3, July 1983, pp. 253-258.
[17] http://www.codesandciphers.org.uk/virtualbp/fish/colossus.htm
[18] e-mail, Tony Sale, 7/12/02.
[19] (Anonymous, *Report*, 49).
[20] (Ecckles, A Trigger, 143-146).
[21] (Michie, *General,* 339).
[22] (Michie, General, 350).
[23] (ibid, 330).
[24] (ibid. 330).
[25] (Flowers, The Design, 246).
[26] (Michie, *General*, 327).

Chapter 9

Complications and Confusions

Background

In the normal operation of the Fish system by the Germans, a number of complications were introduced over the years to bedevil the cryptanalysts at GCHQ. In addition, operational problems on the part of the German operators and intermittent equipment problems added to the woes of the cryptanalysts. All of these things introduced problems that GCHQ had to solve. However, in some cases these problems opened windows leading to solutions for a class of break-ins.

Complications

The Germans diligently made improvements to the security of the Fish system. Primarily these improved security steps were related to the keying procedures and operational discipline. Each of these security improvements was, in turn, detected and ways to overcome them were found by GCHQ.

Fixing the Keying Procedure

The break into the message of August 30, 1941, discussed in Chapter 3, was possible in part because the pin patterns of the S and M wheels consisted of long stretches of ciphertext where the S wheels were ineffective. The result was that the ciphering equation ($Z = P + X +$ constant) was applicable most of the time. Because of the constant, the delta form of the ciphering equation became $\Delta Z = \Delta P + \Delta X$, which greatly simplified the deciphering task.

Also recall that Bill Tutte analyzed Channel 1 and was able to find the pin pattern of that channel. This was possible because the pin pattern was not random. Similar analysis gave the pin patterns of the other four channels.

After August 30, 1941, the Germans evidently sensed that they had a keying problem. To fix this problem they wanted to make sure that no statistical information could be gleaned from the analysis of a single channel of ciphertext. Therefore they made modifications to the design of the pin patterns for all new issue of the keying instructions.[1] By the March-April, 1942 period, these changes were routinely used by the Germans, eliminating any chance of finding statistically useful information in a single channel.

The first step taken by the Germans was to design the key so that the X_i and S_i wheels pin patterns would have approximately equal numbers of 1s and 0s. The result is that the X_i and S_i streams are statistically flat at 0.5 for both 1s and 0s..

The Germans must have recognized that the first difference, Δ, of each of the X and S streams could contain statistically useful information. Therefore, they took a second step to eliminate the use of first differences by the enemy. In other words, they wanted $P[\Delta X = 0] = 0.5$ and $P[\Delta S' = 0] = 0.5$.*

The first differences, Δ, of the X channels were made flat by adjusting the spacing of the 1s and 0s. To this end, the pins of X_i were adjusted so that the number of changes from 1 to 0, 0 to 1, 0 to 0, and 1 to 1 were approximately equal. By making these equal, $P[\Delta X_i = 0] = P[\Delta X_i = 1] = 0.5$.

The design of the S_i wheel pin spacing is a little more difficult because these wheels were stepped in an irregular pattern by the motor wheels. The goal of the S' wheel pin spacing was $P[\Delta S'_i = 1] = 0.5$. It follows also that $P[\Delta S'_i = 0] = .05$.

The two independent conditions for $\Delta S = 1$ are:

1) The S wheels steps. The S wheels step when the total motor wheel† is 1. Let the fraction of 1s in the total motor M = a. Thus the probability of the S wheels stepping is a. Remember that M_{37} is stepped by M_{61} which is stepped on each character.

2) The pins on an S wheels are adjusted so that $P[\Delta S_i = 1] = b_i$..

The probability of these two events occurring is product of the two probabilities.

$$P[\Delta S' = 1] = a\, b_i = a\, P[\Delta S_i = 1]$$

For $P[\Delta S' = 1] = 0.5$, the Germans adjusted the pins of the S and M wheels so that $ab_i = 0.5$. This means that the two motor wheels and all five of the S wheels were adjusted to achieve this condition.

In one example, the M_2 wheel had 11 ones for 37 positions, a = 11/37 = 0.703. From observations of the actual S and M pin patterns, $b_i = 0.7$ giving:

$$ab_i = 0.703 \times 0.7 = 0.492 \approx 0.5.$$

The Germans set the pins according to these requirements and achieved their goal that there would be no statistically useful information in a single channel or the delta of a single channel. However, the Germans must not have perceived what Tutte saw, the possibility of the Double Delta algorithm that evaluated at two channels for statistically useful information. A proof that two channels will yield useful information is found in Appendix D.

The patterns used (after the condition $ab_i = 0.5$ was imposed) were compared to the patterns used with the pattern of the August 30, 1941 and other messages of that year. For these patterns a = 0.703 and $b_i < 0.5$, and ab_i was always less than 0.352.[2] Thus the small amount of obscuring S information made the break into the August 30, 1941message possible.

Key Changing Periods

---

* Recall that S' is the effective pattern after the S wheels are stepped by the motor wheels.

† $M1$ steps on every character. $M2$ steps when $M1 = 1$. The Total Motor is the effective motor dots from $M1$ and $M2$.

Over the life of the deployment of Lorenz, the Germans changed the frequency of changing the keys, the wheel pattern and the wheel setting. Table 9.1shows the pertinent dates and the portion of the keying effected.

Table 9.1 Key Change Periods

Date	*X* Pin Patterns	*S* Pin Patterns	*M* Pin Patterns	X , S, and M Wheel Setting
Start of use	Monthly	3 Months	Daily	Each Message
May 1942 [3]	Monthly	3 Months	Daily	Each Message
October 1942 [4]	Monthly	Monthly	Daily	Each Message
July 1944 [5]	Daily	Daily	Daily	Each Message

These changes in keying periods did not give significant trouble to GCHQ; they were able to keep up. However, the change in the *X* and *S* pin patterns in July 1944 would have been a disaster had it not been for the availability of Colossi with wheel breaking capabilities, described in Chapter 8.*

Changes to Message Serial Number Placement

Early Fish messages, after June 1941, attached the message serial number as a plaintext preamble.[6] The ciphertext message received on August 30, 1941 had its message serial number enciphered in the text. The crib of SPRUNCH... was the key for Col Tiltman to unlock this cipher. The evidence is not clear but it seems that for a period of time, message serial numbers were sent in both plaintext and enciphered.

Michie, Good and Timms write, when referring to the message of August 30, 1941, "The practice of giving the serial number externally and internally had ceased some weeks previously." [7] When referring to the early period when hand methods of wheel setting were used at GCHQ, after March 1942, Michie and Field also write, "This practice of giving the serial number in clear soon ceased." [8]

Therefore, the evolution of the placement of serial numbers was first in plaintext, second in plaintext and ciphertext, and finally in ciphertext only. The dates of these changes have not been established and were probably implemented on different links at different times by the Germans.

Changes to Indicators

The 12 character direct indicators were changed in October 1942 to an indirect method using an indicator number list in the possession of both operators.† This method for signifying to the receiving operator the wheel setting used with a message worked as follows. The originating operator selected a 12-character indicator from a list and transmitted, in plaintext, the letters QEP‡ plus a two-digit pointer to the place in the list with the indicator. The receiving operator would lookup the QEP number on his list and set the receiving Lorenz machine.[9] No evidence has been found of the frequency of indicator list change.

---

* This change occurred just after D-Day and lasted for the duration of the war. The use of the word disaster is not an exaggeration.

† The use of explicit indicators (A, B, C, etc.) represented a possible point of entry for cryptographers; the use of an indirect reference to a list reduced this hazard. However, depth could still be recognized for messages sent on the same day that used the same QEP number.

‡ QSN was used for a short time prior to the use of QEP.

Each end of a link had constant two-way communications over a separate channel or frequency, usually in plaintext. The operators could constantly monitor and report the progress of a transmission. Much of this chitchat was in Q-signals, an abbreviated code that was usually well known by radio operators; QEP numbers is an example. [10]

The QEP message was sent over this parallel link and provided the wheel setting of the next message to be transmitted. Thus Knockholt had to monitor and record the activity on these links as well as the primary links.[11]

Limitations

A limitation was a feature added to the Lorenz that resulted in an additional stepping of the *S* wheels under control of events other than the *M* wheels. The effect of limitations was to override the normal stepping of the *S* wheels as controlled by the *M* wheels. There are three versions of limitations. As these limitations were introduced, the older ones remained in effect and the action was the mod2 sum of the limitations in effect. [12]

The first version was called an X2-oneback limitation. This limitation steps the *S* wheels one position whenever the previous (called one back) X_2 wheel pin was a one. This limitation was first seen on the Herring link between Rome and Tunis in March 1943.[13]

The second form of limitation was the P5–twoback that steps the *S* wheels when the plaintext channel P_5 two back (previous + one) was a one. This limitation appeared briefly in March and April 1943. The use was discontinued, and then was fully implemented on all links in December 1943. This limitation gave the Germans more trouble than anticipated and its use was finally dropped in January 1944. This limitation was a form of Autokey or, as called at GCHQ, Autoclave. The problems experienced by the Germans are characteristic of an Autokey. That is, an error in Channel 5 propagates through the balance of the message requiring a resend. This not only required time on the part of the operators to resend messages but gave GCHQ an opening to the ciphertext because the resends could provided depth. The problems with Autokey or Autoclave were described by F. Pratt in 1942. [14]

The third limitation used by The Germans was S1-oneback. As its name implies, the output of the S_1 wheel, one back, was used to step the *S* wheels.[15]

Limitations were first detected by GCHQ when two messages with the same indicators would not respond as they should to anagramming. Much effort was devoted to solving the problems introduced by limitations. Limitations, although a serious problem for a period of time, were mastered at GCHQ.

Confusions

Confusions were operational problems inadvertently created by German operators that usually provided an opening for GCHQ personnel to break into a Fish message. The evidence suggests that these confusions were beneficial to GCHQ for breaking and settings the *S* and *M* wheels on current traffic after the initial work of *X* wheel breaking and setting had been achieved.

Go-Backs

A go-back was an operational problem caused when the receiving operator signals that the message was not being received after a transmission had commenced.[16] A timing diagram of a go-back is shown in Figure 9.1. Albert Small described go-backs.

> "The German sender, when interrupted by a request for a resend, stops his machine just where it is, moves the tape back from six to ten inches, and starts the machine again.* This means that there will be from sixty to one hundred letters of perfect repeat in the plain text. These go-backs are recognizable because of the pause in sending as the tape is being adjusted. The difficulty is in finding how one part fits onto the other. In practice this is done by breaking into each other and fitting the plain texts together." [17]

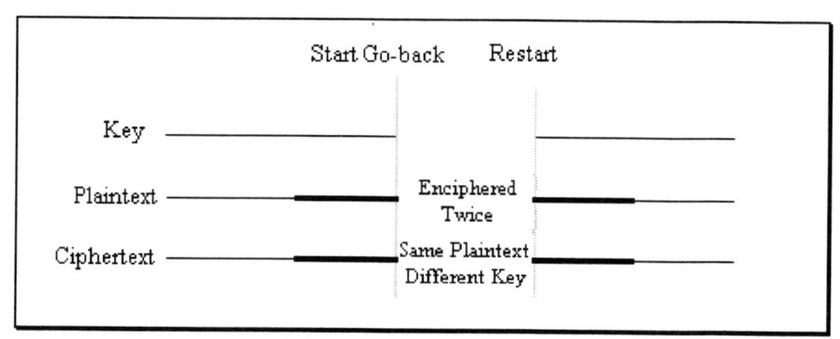

Figure 9.1 Go-backs

A go-back means that GCHQ had two identical segments of plaintext that were enciphered by different keytexts. This is the opposite of the August 30, 1941 situation where there were two different ciphertext with the same keytext. Even though the situation is different, the same technique is used to find the *X* wheel patterns. Adding the two segments of ciphertext gives the sum of the two keytexts. A special machine named Aquarius was built to assist in fitting the segments together around a go-back (Chapter 10).

Slides

Slides were not German operational problems. They were the insertion of extraneous letters or the omission of letters from the body of the ciphertext.[18] Slides were created by mistakes at the Knockholt receiving station and required extensive checking of the intercept tapes before they were released to GCHQ.

Because there was redundancy in recording intercepts (two operators independently punched paper tapes from the recorded the undulator tape), extensive checking could be done. There were about 50 people on each watch to perform quality checking tasks. Even so, slides were counted in the finished ciphertext tapes and the elimination of slides was not complete; about one slide per 16,000 characters was the achieved quality level.

---

* As discussed in Chapter 2, the Fish channels were full duplex with continuous bidirection communications between operators.

Broken Tape

Occasionally, the plaintext tape on the sending Lorenz machine would break or for some other reason the plaintext tape would run out and create blanks in the plaintext. If the *X* wheel patterns had been known, then over the stretch of ciphertext, stretches of pure *S'* could be recovered. [19] The Newmanry provided the keytext, *X*, to the Testery. By subtracting *X* from the received ciphertext *Z*, *S'* can be found.

$$Z = X \oplus S' \oplus P \text{ and as } P = 0$$
$$S' = X \oplus Z.$$

This stretch of available pure *S'* continued until the operator stopped the Lorenz machine and corrected the problem. With stretches of *S'*, the settings of *S* and the *M* wheels could be found as described in Chapter 6.

Stuck Tape

Sometimes the plaintext tape on the sending Lorenz machine got stuck and did not advance. When this happened, one letter was repeatedly enciphered until the operator fixed the problem. A pause in the transmission occurred while this problem was being fixed, a pause that was duly reported in the log from Knockholt.[20]

By examining all 32 possible characters that the tape could have stuck on, the cryptanalysts in the Newmanry could identify pure *S'*. The technique was the same as with a broken tape except that the stuck-on character had to be found.

References

[1] Anonymous, *Report on British Attack on "FISH"*, Communications Intelligence Technical Paper TS 47, Navy Department, Washington D.C., May 1945, NARA RG 457, Box 607, Pg. 25.
[2] Michie, D., Good, J., Timms, G., *General Report on Tunny*, 1945, Released to the Public Record Office in 2000, http://www.alanturing.net/tunny_report, Pg. 306.
[3] (ibid. 308).
[4] (ibid. 320).
[5] (ibid. 319).
[6] (ibid. 297).
[7] (ibid. 299).
[8] (ibid. 304).
[9] (ibid. 320).
[10] (Anonymous, *Report*, 14).
[11] (ibid. 14).
[12] (ibid. 7).
[13] (Michie, *General*, 323).
[14] Pratt, F., *Secret and Urgent, The Story of Codes and Ciphers*, Blue Ribbon Books, N.Y., 1942, pp 205-297.
[15] (Anonymous, *Report* , 7).
[16] Small, A. *Special Fish Report,* NARA, NR 4628 Box 1417, also http://www.codesandciphter.org.uk/documents/small/page112.htm, December 1944, Pg. 63.
[17](Anonymous, *Report*, 82).
[18] (ibid. 18).
[19] (Small, *Special*, 73).
[20] (ibid. 73).

Chapter 10

Special Machines

Background

In addition to the Heath Robinsons and Colossi, a number of special purpose machines were designed and constructed for GCHQ for special tasks.

Because breaking into the Fish ciphertext was a statistical process, significant processing power and tape handling equipment was needed. Debate began within GCHQ whether to add special function attachments called gadgets to Colossus or to design and construct special machines. Examples of these gadgets are the rectangling gadget and the subtraction gadget, both explained in Chapter 8. The addition of gadgets to Colossus was preferred by some rather than adding special machines.[1] With Colossus, operator and maintenance training could be standardized at reduced cost.

The counter argument for special machines viewed them as necessary for such specialized tasks that the addition of gadgets to Colossi was deemed to be an ineffective use of resources. Finally, GCHQ did a little of both, gadgets for Colossus and special machines. Only a few of these special machines were actually built.

Most of the special machines described in this chapter were located in the Newmanry where all machine aided wheel breaking and setting was performed. However, these machines supported Heath Robinson and Colossus. Tunny decoding machines were assigned to the Testery where the need for decrypting existed.

Tunny

By April 1942, breaking into the Fish messages had been so successful that the decision was made to design and construct functional analogs of the Lorenz cipher machine. The first of these machines, named Tunny, was in operation in June 1942.

Design and construction of Tunny was performed by the Post Office Research Station at Dollis Hill, a major support arm of GCHQ for specialized equipment. Sid Broadhurst, an experienced designer of automatic telephone circuits, headed the design team.[2] The evolution of Tunny proceeded down two paths:[3]

1) Machines for straight deciphering of a ciphertext with known wheel patterns and wheel settings. These machines were used in the Testery and were called "Decoding Machines." Thirteen were in use at the end of the war.
2) Enhancements to aid in the Newmanry in wheel setting and breaking. Three of these machines were in service at the end of the war.

Tunny Decoding Machine Design

Recall from Chapter 2 that the Lorenz machine generated the key stream by mechanical means. The designers of Tunny were telephone engineers and by training and experience were inclined to use stepping switches and relays in their designs.* A

---

* The use of stepping switches is reminiscent of the Japanese Purple machine and its American analog.

photograph of a stepping switch is shown in Figure 10.1. The rotors of the switch are stepped by the relays shown at the top left of the figure. Electrical connections were made to the stationary contact and the stepping switches could be wired as analogs of the Lorenz pin wheels.

Figure 10.1 Stepping Switch

A photograph of three Tunny Decoding machines is shown in Figure 10.2. A bank of plugs represented the 12 Lorenz wheels with each of their pin positions. When the wheel pin patterns had been found, 501 plug points were set to either a one or a zero. As the stepping switches stepped, the *X* and *S* patterns were generated under the control of the M_1 and M_2 stepping switches.

Figure10.2 Three Tunny Decoding Machines
(The National Archives, London)

Although a U.S. built Purple Machine was given to Bletchley Park in 1941, there is no evidence that it influenced the selection of stepping switches for Tunny.

Tunny operated in much the same way as a Lorenz by a German operator deciphering a ciphertext message. The machine was set up with the correct wheel patterns and wheel settings, and then an operator typed the ciphertext with the teleprinter. Just as with the operation of the Lorenz, the output of the *X* and *S* wheel analogues were added to the cipher characters and the plaintext was typed out on another teleprinter. It is assumed that there was a second teleprinter and that the operation was similar to the Hand Mode shown in Figure 2.4. Ciphertext on punched tape could also be input to Tunny. [4]

The output of Tunny was German plaintext. It was necessary, therefore, for the output to be translated and cleaned up to correct any garbles. The teleprinters that recorded the output were modified so that the control codes, shown in Table 1.2, would not be responsive, and the symbols would be printed. In other words, the code 01000 would print 4, not perform a line feed. Interpretation of these codes was left to the translators.

Design and construction of the Tunny machine was ordered in April 1942 and the first unit was delivered to GCHQ in June 1942. This is an incredible achievement. Approximately two years after the first whispers of a new cipher system were heard, a faithful analog of the cipher device was delivered and placed in service at Bletchley Park.

Because the Colossi had special triggers that were convenient to set up, Colossus was used to emulate the Lorenz machine and reduced the need for Tunnies. However, in May 1945, thirteen decoding machine Tunnies were in service, three of which are shown in Figure 10.2. [5]

Newmanry Tunnies

Tasks to which these machines were placed were: 1) generate pseudo plaintext *D* tapes from Colossus output, 2) test tapes for *X* and *S* wheel testing, and 3) basic Motor tapes required for printing the motor pattern.[6] There is little information available today on these machines. [7]

Only three of these machines were constructed and it appears that they were upgraded and modified on site to provide general support in managing paper tape for the Newmanry.

Dragon

The purpose of Dragon was to find stretches of *S*' text. This was done with a common crib *P* of up to 10 letters in a given pseudo plaintext *D* so that $P + D = S'$.* The input to the system was the *D* or de-chi tape. The crib was setup with switches and "dragged" through the pseudo text. The characters were added giving characters of *S*'. Once S' was known, the stretching could be removed giving *S*.

Dragon performed the same function of finding stretches of *S*' as described in Section 6.1 except that the sought for crib was in *D* not in ΔD. There were two Dragons in use in the Testery in May 1945.

There is a delightful story told by Gil Hayward about Dragon.[8] Hayward writes that the first Dragon was built in the U.S. and taken to GCHQ in the summer of 1944 by U.S. Army Sgt. Tom Collins. This machine worked poorly, if at all, and was finally

---

* See Chapter 6 on Finding S' and Motor Wheels.

replaced by a version built at Dollis Hill by Sid Broadhurst. Hayward wrote that the name Dragon was, in part, due to the chomping noises that Sgt. Collins' machine made when operating.* Another U.S. built Dragon is mentioned that was used for short cribs.[9]

Two Dragons were in service in the Testery and one was under construction in May 1945.[10]

Proteus

Proteus was designed to find the enciphering keytext characters when two messages were enciphered with the same key (having the same indicators), that is, a depth of two. This is the same problem that Col. Tiltman unraveled when breaking into the message of August 30, 1941 (Chapter 3).

The basic strategy of Proteus used a crib of up to six letters in ciphertext along with a dictionary of several hundred words that could possibly be the crib word in plaintext. An exhaustive search of the word list was then made to see if a word matched the enciphered crib. The operation is illustrated with a one-character example.

Assume that a character of plaintext 1 is M, and the corresponding character of plaintext 2 is R, and the unknown key character is K. The enciphering process gives two corresponding ciphertext characters are W and S.

$$\text{Ciphertext Z1} = M \oplus K = 00111 \oplus 11110 = 11001 \text{ (W)}$$
$$\text{Ciphertext Z2} = R \oplus K = 01010 \oplus 11110 = 10100 \text{ (S)}$$

The ciphertext characters are all that is known to the cryptanalyst. Adding, mod2, the two ciphertext characters eliminates the key character giving the value Φ.†

$$\Phi = W \oplus S = 11001 \oplus 10100 = 01101$$

Assume that a cryptanalyst has selected the plaintext crib of M, believed to be in one of the plaintext messages. What is the corresponding plaintext in the other message? Also assume that the list of potential cribs, held in the dictionary, consists of the characters, P, R, and S.

The crib M is added to the characters from the dictionary and Φ. The following sequence of operations is performed:

1. $M \oplus P \oplus \Phi = 00111 \oplus 01101 \oplus 01101 = 00111$
2. $M \oplus R \oplus \Phi = 00111 \oplus 01010 \oplus 01101 = 00000$
3. $M \oplus S \oplus \Phi = 00111 \oplus 10100 \oplus 01101 = 11110$

We see that at step 2, the result of this operation is 00000 or /. This result identifies the dictionary character R (01010) is the plaintext character enciphered with the keytext character K The keytext character can now be found by:

---

* There is no report on the problems with, or the fate of, the Dragon sent from the U.S. to GCHQ in American reports.

† This process is described in Chapter 3.

Key = Z2 $\oplus$ R = 10100 $\oplus$ 01010 = 11101 (K)
And
Key = Z1 $\oplus$ M = 11001 $\oplus$ 00111 = 11110 (K)

The Proteus machine would have stopped on Step 2 when / was encountered and would display the letter R. Because up to seven letters were in the crib and the dictionary, a stop would only occur when all characters were /.

Obviously a single character, as in this illustration, would not provide useful results. However, the six-character crib plus a dictionary of several hundred common words would have been effective for the Proteus function.

The documentation on Proteus does not describe its implementation in any detail. It can assumed that the two ciphertexts were read from two paper tapes off line and added to give Φ. The Φ characters were then read into Proteus from a Colossus-like bedstead. The crib was set up on a plug-panel that was cycled by thyratron rings, as were the keys on Colossus, Figures 8.3 and 8.4. Proteus exploited Colossus technology with little need for new component or circuit engineering.

It is not known how many Proteus machines, if any, were built. Michie, Good, and Timms write that only one was under construction in May, 1945.[11] Ciphertext messages with depth of two probably became rare as the Germans tightened up their security and the need for this special machine did not materialize.

Aquarius

The purpose of Aquarius was to set go-backs in ΔD text (Chapter 9). With go-backs, a string of ΔD text is compared to a portion of the same text. In this way the demarcation between the last good ΔD before the go-back and the characters after the enciphering process was restarted could be identified.

The Aquarius function was implemented with storage of 315 five-bit characters in the machine. This memory was implemented using capacitors storing charge for each bit. The bits were refreshed at least every two minutes, an early use of a dynamic RAM.*

The ΔD tape was read into the Aquarius in one pass. The last 218 characters before the go-back and the first 97 characters after the go-back were stored in the capacitor memory. The reason for these strange numbers is unknown but is probably due to some peculiarity of using standard telephone components for the implementation.

The characters after the go-back were shifted backward until there was an overlap of characters before the go-back, the last 11 and the first 11. These characters were processed as described in the following paragraphs. The overlap was increased to 12, then 13 and so on. After the overlap reached 97, the shifting back continued until the 218th character before the go-back was being compared with the first character after the go-back.

The processing of these characters is based of the fact that with a go-back there are two segments of the same plaintext that has been enciphered with different keytext.

---

* The first use of capacitors for binary storage, known to the author, was by John Atanasoff in the late 1930s

This is the opposite of normal depth where two different plaintexts are enciphered with the same keytext. Aquarius processed ΔD rather than P because of greater statistical variations. For the ΔS before the go back (a) and after the go back (b), at the correct overlap, adding the two ΔS gives:

$$\Delta D(\mathrm{a}) \oplus \Delta D(\mathrm{b}) = \Delta P(\mathrm{a}) \oplus \Delta S'(\mathrm{a}) \oplus \Delta P(\mathrm{b}) \oplus \Delta S'(\mathrm{b}),$$

because the plaintext is the same,

$$\Delta P(\mathrm{a}) = \Delta P(\mathrm{b})$$

Thus

$$\Delta D(\mathrm{a}) \oplus \Delta D(\mathrm{b}) = \Delta S'(\mathrm{a}) \oplus \Delta S'(\mathrm{b}).$$

A count of $[\Delta D(\mathrm{a}) \oplus \Delta D(\mathrm{b})] = 1$ was made for each of the overlap steps. Because $\Delta D(\mathrm{a}) \oplus \Delta D(\mathrm{b})$ resembles the pattern of a $\Delta S'(\mathrm{a}) \oplus \Delta S'(\mathrm{b})$ the count indicates the point of overlap and the point at which the go back should be joined.

Michie and Good write that one Aquarius was "on test" in May 1945.[12] Finding the point of overlap of a go-back was probably done quicker by manual means. We can conclude that, though interesting, there was no real pressure to have even one Aquarius in operation before the war ended.

Mrs. Miles *

Mrs. Miles made tapes for crib runs and prepared tapes for Garbo rectangling, described in the next section. This special machine was designed without the use of binary memory of any kind. [13]

The requirement to prepare tapes for Garbo presented a unique challenge. The challenge was to read a ciphertext tape and compute Z⊕s from widely different locations on the tape. These values were to be punched into another tape for Garbo. This operation is equivalent to a modern "gather" operation that is performed in random access memory. However, tape is a sequential memory and is not suited to this operation.

How was requirement not to use memory to be accomplished with mechanical paper tape readers that read one character at a time?

This requirement was craftily solved by using five tape readers with the ciphertext Z tape passing through each reader in turn. For the example of a 11,000 character ciphertext and a 1,271 key (X_1 and X_2), there is a loop of 2,542 Z⊕ characters between each tape reader (TR) as shown in Figure 10.3.

* Sometimes called just Miles.

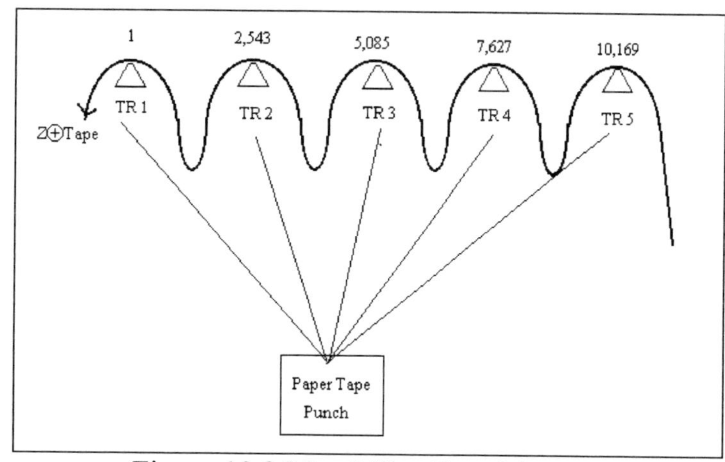

Figure 10.3 Mrs. Miles Tape Memory

The loop between tape readers was a function of the length of the ciphertext tape and the number of bits, 5, in the Baudot code. That is:

Loop = Next highest multiple of 1271 of the remainder when the length of the ciphertext tape divided by 5.

For example, the loop for a ciphertext of 12,710 characters is 12,710 ÷ 5 = 2,542 characters. For an 11,000 character ciphertext, the loop is also 2,542 characters.

At each of the five reading stations, Mrs. Miles performed the Double Delta on two channels, for example $\Delta Z_1 \oplus \Delta Z_2 = Z\oplus$. The five $Z\oplus$s were punched into another tape that was input to Garbo, described in the next section. Figure 10.4 indicates the address at which $Z\oplus$ was being computed and punched at the same time for a 12,710 character ciphertext.

	Time 1	Time 2	Time 3	Time 4	....	Time 2542
TR 1	1	2	3	4	....	2,542
TR 2	2,543	2,544	2,545	2,546	....	5,084
TR 3	5,085	5,087	5,088	5,089	....	7,626
TR 4	7,627	7,628	7,629	7,630	....	10,168
TR 5	10,169	10, 170	10,171	10,172	....	12,710

Figure 10.4 Tape Reader Characters

Mrs. Miles had a paper tape punch. At Time 1, the paper tape punch records the punch/no punch of the five addresses shown under Time 1 in the table. At Time 2, the next five values were punched into the tape. This continued until the entire Z tape is read and the tape for Garbo had been punched.

What had been accomplished is that the 12,710 values of $Z\oplus$ had been collapsed into 2,542 five bit characters. These are not Baudot characters but characters that represent 0-5 values of $Z\oplus$. The characters are not encoded in any way.

The system consisted of five Western Union tape readers* and two reperforators plus relay logic.† Because of the relatively slow paper tape readers, relay logic was fast enough. However, it seems that relay logic was used for Mrs. Miles I and II. Mrs. Miles III used vacuum tube logic, probably of Colossus design, requiring approximately 70 tubes.

There is a hint in the Small report that each of the tape readers had the logical capability to perform the double delta at each of the five tape readers. If this is the case, the tape input to Mrs. Miles was not a tape of Z⊕s but could have been all five characters of Z plus the keytext *X* tape with the calculation of Z⊕ being performed on Mrs. Miles.

Michie and Good indicate that there were three Mrs. Miles in operation in May 1945. Evidently this special machine provided a useful support role for other machines as well as the Colossus. Miles IV, under construction at the end of the war, was largely electronic.

Garbo

This special machine was used primarily to help in the construction of rectangles and may have been used to test ideas before incorporation on Colossus as gadgets. [14] Garbo was to print *Z*⊕s in a format so that a clerk could easily create a rectangle without scanning a linearly printed version, such as found in Figure 5.4.

A Garbo had two IBM paper tape readers, one IBM typewriter and one paper tape punch.

Garbo I had a small relay memory. The Δ form of a ciphertext or keytext tape could be computed by reading one tape and using the memory to save the last character. Or, two tapes could be read offset by one character. It is not known whether the Xor functions needed for Δs was relay logic or vacuum tube, as with Colossus. Because of the relatively low speeds involved, the logic was probably implemented with relays.

Garbo could delta either characters or selected channels. It could also Double Delta two channels. The output of a delta run could be either punched into paper tape or printed. If punched, the speed was probably 50 characters per second, while if printed only 10 characters per second. A printed delta of a 10,000 character tape would require about 17 minutes.

The control of Garbo was designed so that the five channels of a paper tape could be permuted; any character could be printed as any other character on the typewriter. The purpose of this feature is not disclosed in the available references.

The first format for printing *Z*⊕ to support rectangling worked in the following way. The printing width was set to the width of the smaller of the two wheels: 31 for a rectangle of Channel 1 and 2. Thirty one characters of *Z*⊕ were printed followed by as many carriage returns as the depth of the stack, plus a few. After 41 of these spaced lines were printed, the run was stopped and the paper in the typewriter was set back so that the next set of 1,271 characters could be printed below the first set. This process continued until the complete set of *Z*⊕ had been printed.

---

* Western Union tape readers were supplied under Lend Lease to the UK.

† Reperforators are also known as paper tape punches.

A clerk could take this printed version of $Z\oplus$ and fill in a rectangle with surplus-deficit information reading diagonally down and to the right. The rectangle thus developed would be used to find ΔX and X as described in Chapter 5. For a $Z\oplus$ tape of 12,710 characters, 310 line of typed output would be produced. This output could be confusing and a source of error.

Another printing format for Garbo was developed later to reduce the opportunity for confusion with the first format. This operation required a special tape prepared on Mrs. Miles, as described previously. The tape had been punched so instead of carrying Baudot coded information; the five positions of each "character" were punched according to the value of $Z\oplus$ as shown in Figure 10.5. Instead of calling the rows of punches "channels" they were called "levels." The entry in each cell of Figure 10.3 is the address of a $Z\oplus$. For an 11,000 character $Z\oplus$ tape, the entries are as follows,

Level 1	1	2	. . . . . .	1,271	. . . . . .	2,542
Level 2	2,543	2,544	. . . . . .	3,813	. . . . . .	5,084
Level 3	5,086	5,087	. . . . . .	6,355	. . . . . .	7,626
Level 4	7,327	7,628	. . . . . .	8,897	. . . . . .	10,168
Level 5	10,169	10,170	. . . . . .	11,000	END	

Figure 10.5 Mrs. Miles $Z\oplus$ Tape[15]

This tape is 2,542 characters in length. Garbo starts reading the tape, from the left of Figure 10.1 and looks at each character in turn. The characters were analyzed for the number of ones they contained and the result printed in a code.

If the character is / there were no ones and 0 was printed. If the character has one 1 (found in E, 4, 9, 3, and T) a 1 was printed. Likewise, a character with 2 ones resulted in the printing of 2 and so on. In other words, Garbo had made counts of the number of ones in the rectangle cells and printed the count. From this printout a surplus-deficit count could be made.

The input from the example of Figure 5.4 is shown in Figure 10.6 (the entries are the character numbers). This example has a keytext length of 15 and a ciphertext length of 60.

Level 1	1	2	3	4	. . . . . .	12
Level 2	13	14	15	16	. . . . . .	24
Level 3	25	26	27	28	. . . . . .	36
Level 4	37	38	39	40	. . . . . .	48
Level 5	49	50	51	51	. . . . . .	60

Figure 10.6 Example Mrs. Miles $Z\oplus$ Tape

From the printout, it is a relative simple matter to convert the count of ones to a surplus-deficit value and post the results to a rectangle, writing down the diagonal.

Junior

Chapter 6 described how a printed pseudo plaintext (de-chi) tape was used to break the *S'* wheels and find *S*. The pseudo plaintext *D* was computed on a Colossus but would not be printed because of the speed mismatch between Colossus and its printer. However, paper tape punches operated at about 100 characters per second, thus it was best to punch rather than print the pseudo plaintext *D*.

Junior was a simple machine that printed the pseudo plaintext tape off-line from the Colossus. This special machine had one paper tape reader, one Electromatic typewriter and various switches and plug boards to control the machine.[16]

Michie and Good indicate that in May 1945 there were four Juniors in the building named Block F.

Angel

There is only a brief mention of Angel, a machine for copying tapes. [17] The bedsteads of Heath Robinson and Colossus were hard on tapes and several copies of all tapes were prepared and rigorously checked before issue. Special operations were performed on some tapes. For example, the start and stop holes were hand punched with a special punch. Tapes for Mrs. Miles were carefully measured and marked for positioning in the five tape readers. At the end of the war, four Angels were in operation in the Newmanry. [18]

References

[1] Michie, D., Good, J., Timms, G., *General Report on Tunny*, 1945, Released to the Public Record Office in 2000, http://www.alanturing.net/tunny_report, pg. 330.

[2] Hayward, G. "Operation Tunny", *Codebreakers*, ed. Hinsley and Stripp, Oxford University Press, 1993, pg. 176.

[3](Michie, *General*, 376).

[4] Halton, K., "The Tunny Machine", *Codebreakers, The Inside Story of Bletchley Park,* Ed. Hinsley, F. H., Stripp, A., Oxford University Press, 1993, pg. 170.

[5] (Michie, *General*, 327).

[6] (ibid. 286).

[7] (ibid. 376).

[8] Hayward, Operation, 184).

[9] Anonymous, *Report on British Attack on "FISH",* Communications Intelligence Technical Paper TS 47, Navy Department, Washington D.C., May 1945, NARA RG 457, Box 607, pg. 84.

[10] (Michie, *General*, 327).

[11] (ibid. 327).

[12] (ibid. 327).

[13] Small, A. *Special Fish Report,* NARA, NR 4628 Box 1417, also http://www.codesandciphter.org.uk/documents/small/page112.htm, December 1944, pg 107.

[14] (ibid. 105).

[15] (ibid. 105).

[16] (ibid. 105).

[17] (Michie, *General*, 285).

[18] (ibid. 327).

Appendix A

Chronology

Date	Event
1918	Vernam patent issued
1920	Morehouse patent issued
1920	Room 40 activity renamed Government Code and Cipher School
1931	U.S. Army given a ten rotor ITT machine designed by Parker Hitt. Broken in short order by Signal Intelligence Section.
August 1939	Government Code and Cipher School moved from London to Bletchley Park and renamed the Government Communications Headquarters (GCHQ).
Second Half, 1940	First heard non-Morse signals
February 1941	End of Hellschreiber signals
May 1941	Tutte starts at Bletchley Park
May 1941	Jack Good joined Bletchley Park
After June, 1941	Teleprinter signals received in garbled form
Middle 1941	German radio link, Vienna-Athens with Schlusselzusatz, SZ 40/42
30 August 1941	Message of 3,976 characters sent and resent
January 1942	The GCHQ understood method of operation of the Army Machine (Tunny)
Beginning 1942	Post Office asked to produce a Tunny
Spring 1942	Hand breaking of Athens-Vienna link
Early 1942	Started Statistical approach. 0s predominated over 1s in the 5th impulse of Tunny
March 1942	Message setting theory attempted based on indicators.
March-April, 1942	Germans arranged that ab = 1/2. Thus no statistical information from one channel.
March, 1942	Theory of indicators confirmed
April 1942	Decision to make some machines (Tunnies)
May 1942	Use of indicators for breaking the wheels
June 1942	First Tunny in operation
18 July 1942	Current traffic read for first time
July 1942	Work on Tunny by Research Section moved to Tunny Section
Mid 1942	Knockholt came on-line
October 1942	Tunny closed down. Codfish and Octopus came into operation using OSN later QEP numbers rather than 12 letter indicators
November 1942	Introduction of QSN's later QEP's ended indicator method
Second 1/2 1942	Hand technique doing OK
November 1942	1st operational link broken. Berlin to Army Group F in Balkans

November 1942	Double Delta Algorithm invented by Bill Tutte
Dec. 1942- May 1943	Herring link, Rome – Tunis, active
December 1942	Max Newman given the job of developing machine methods of wheel setting
January 1943	Broke Army Group C in Rome to Panzer Army in Tunisia
February1943	Management at GCHQ decreed that work on Robinsons should continue and have first priority as unlikely that the tube Colossus would be ready before the end of the war
February 1943	X2-oneback limitation appeared
March 1943	Autoclave used on one link then abandoned
March 1943	Colossus design started
April 1943	Heath Robinson and Tunny delivered to Newmanry
April 1943	Army Group South to Berlin found and broken. Full details of Kursk salient battle in Russia were deciphered
May 1943	Jack Good transferred to Hut F to work on Tunny
May 1943	Newmanry decoded over 1,400,000 letters during the month
May 1943	Links Army Group A to Memel and German mission to Romania Only 1 Robinson available
July 1943	6 German Army Tunny links identified
July 1943	Max Newman formed his section, the Newmanry
Summer, 1943	Links found and broken, Army Group Center to Army Group F in Belgrade
Summer 1943	Germans reduced the number of dots in Bream Mu37 from 22 to 16
September 1943	Allen Coombs joined Colossus team
September 1943	First Robinson completed and waiting to be made to work prior to installation at Bletchley Park
September 1943	First Colossus, Mark I design complete and approaching manufacture
November 1943	*S* wheels set by hand
December 1943	Colossus Mark I demonstrated , Coombs started working on Mark II
December 1943	George Vergin (American) posted to Newmanry
December 1943	X2oneback and P5twoback reinstalled. Production by Testery dried up
December, 1943	Autoclave introduced
January 1944	Gil Hayward posted to BP from North Africa
February 1944	Colossus I arrived at BP
February 1944	Serious interruptions in decrypts
February 1944	Bream chis broken with help from Colossus MK I M37 dotage = 19 X2oneback + P5twoback problem solved
February 1944	Introduction of a German Security device ??
February 1944	Berlin to Field Marshal Gerd von Rundstedt link found, Jellyfish
February 1944	Lorenz machines further modified for security

Early 1944	26 Tunny links each with own cipher settings
Early 1944 (March?)	Decision to made to construct a number of Tunnies
June 1944	Triple limitation: X2oneback + PSI'1oneback + P5twoback
Summer 1944	Daily wheel changes introduced
August 1944	Daily wheel changes coped with and production was higher than ever
Autumn 1944	X2oneback + 5Ptwoback dropped on Western links
October 1944	Serious interruptions in decrypts
November 1944	6 Colossi operating
May 1945	Ten Colossi, two Robinsons and thirteen Decoding Machines operational. Two Robinsons were nearly complete

Appendix B

Breaking the Parker Hitt Cipher Machine

Background

Col. Parker Hitt, U.S. Army Retired, was employed by the I.T.& T. Corporation to design a cipher machine in the mid 1930's for use in secure teleprinter communications.[1] The Hitt design employed a set of ten pinwheels, which generated a key text in the spirit of the Vernam and Morehouse patents.* The key characters were added mod2 to the plaintext to give the ciphertext.

Wheels 1 and 2 enciphered channel 1 of the plaintext, wheels 3 and 4 enciphered channel 2 and so on. Wheel 1 had 96 pin positions; wheel 2 had 97 pin positions, increasing by one for each wheel, with wheel 10 having 105 pin positions. Unlike the Lorenz, the pin patterns were set at the time of manufacture and the pattern could not be changed. All ten wheels stepped as each plaintext character was entered. The length of the keytext cycle was $10.4 \times 10^{19.}$

The enciphering equation of the machine was similar to that of the Lorenz. The outputs of two wheels, K_1 and K_2 were Xor together to give K_{r1}. K_{r1} then Xor with the plaintext bit P_1 to give the ciphertext bit C_1.†

$$K_{r1} = K_1 \oplus K_2$$
$$C_1 = K_{r1} \oplus P_1$$
$$C_1 = K_1 \oplus K_2 \oplus P_1$$

The only security was provided by selecting the starting position of the ten wheels; the pins could not be patterned. To set the wheels, each wheel had the 26 letters of the alphabet on their periphery giving $26^{10} = 1.4 \times 10^{14}$ possible unique starting positions or settings. In the discussion to follow, the wheel setting is called the "key." The key was known to the receiving operator so that the receiving machine could be set to decipher the message. The evidence available today does not describe how the keys were distributed, as indicators with the message or distributed from a central source.

The keying procedure, designed by Col. Hitt, restricted the key to ten-letter words taken from an English Dictionary; random selection of characters for the key was not permitted.

In November 1931, the U.S. Department of State asked the Chief Signal Officer of the Signal Corps to test the security of this machine.[2] The ground rules were set by the Chief Signal Officer. Sixteen messages were enciphered on the machine by the Department of State using their usual instructions and keying procedures. Twelve of these messages would be ordinary Department of State traffic and would each be enciphered with a different key. The keys would not be given to the Chief Signal Officer.

---

* The wheels had notches, not pins as with Lorenz.

† The symbols used in Appendix B are those of reference ii.

Breaking into this system was easily accomplished by a group under W. F. Friedman, F. B. Rowlett, S. Kullback and A. Sinkov. The group was provided with a machine and the pattern of the wheels was quickly found using a method provided by I. T. & T. The belief was that a machine would be captured by an enemy who would quickly uncover its construction and wheel patterns. Thus hiding the machine's construction was not a vital consideration.

This was not the case with the Lorenz cipher machine; a Lorenz was not captured until late in the war. Capture was unlikely because of its deployment to interior lines. As discussed in Chapter 3, the wheel design was understood at GCHQ by analysis of a single German cipher message, not by capture

Solution Where a Portion of the Plaintext is Known

The first group of messages, 10 in number, was attacked using a plaintext crib. The team knew that the last six letters of a Department of State message ended with:

Figure(UC)-M-Letter(LC)-Figure(UC)-J-Letter(LC).

In plaintext these characters are: 5, M, 8, 5, J, 8.* Thus a strong crib was afforded into the ciphertext message. When this ending portion of a message was enciphered using the keytext shown in Table B.1, the resulting ciphertext characters were N, M, T, Q, W, O. Mod2 addition was used as with the Lorenz. The message first analyzed had a total length of 175 characters.

Table B.1 ITT Example 1.

Plaintext		Keytext	Ciphertext	
Figures(UC)	11011	11101	N	00110
M (full stop)	00111	00000	M	00111
Letters (C)	11111	11110	T	00001
Figures(UC)	11010	00110	Q	11101
J (,)	11010	00011	W	11001
Letters(LC)	11111	11100	O	00011

The task was to find the key, or wheel settings, that would yield the key knowing only the ciphertext and the crib. The last six characters of the ciphertext were added mod2 to the crib (the assumed plaintext). The result was an assumed keytext. The first bit string of the assumed key text, from earliest to last, was 101001. This string was generated by the Xor of wheels 1 and 2 of the machine. By trial and error, wheels 1 and 2 were positioned until the assumed keytext string was identified.

These two wheels were then backed up 175 - 6 = 169 steps to a tentative starting position. If this starting position had two characters that could be a digraph of a 10 character key word (something like ZQ could not be part of a common English word), they were accepted as tentatively correct.

The time taken for these trial and error searches is not revealed. However, to exhaustively try the $26 \times 26 = 676$ possible combinations would take many hours. At five minutes per try, almost 60 hours would be required. A brute force exhaustive search was

* See Table 1.2. The control codes symbols (8, 5, etc.) are those used by GCHQ, not those used at the time with the ITT cipher machine.

not used. Rather a sorting procedure reduced the amount of work required. Rowlett reports that all of ten test messages were broken in a day and one half.[3]

The analysis continued with the other wheels until the correct 10 character key word was uncovered. By the time four or six characters had been deciphered, the complete key word could probably be guessed by reference to a dictionary.

Solution Without Knowledge of Any Plaintext

The idea for solving this cipher was to select two characters that would be legitimate digraphs of a key word, and then decipher some of the ciphertext and test to see if the resulting plaintext was statistically probable.

The Signal Intelligence Service under Friedman had made extensive investigations into the letter frequency characteristics of English and other languages.[4] The observation was made that for War Department English plaintext, the weighted values for Channel #1 was 0.363 for 1s and 0.647 for 0s. Table B.2 shows the frequencies for all five of the channels.

Table B.2 War Department English

Channel	1	0
1	.363	.637
2	.358	.642
3	.518	.482
4	.360	.640
5	.326	.674

From this table we see that any channel, other than #3, has a statistical bias toward zeros and can serve to test tentative decipherments. In the report, the following test case was presented as shown in Table B.3 and B.4.

An example of ciphertext is shown in Table B.3. The first column shows the first 20 characters of the ciphertext. The corresponding Baudot codes are shown in the second column. The process started with a crib. The last two characters of a key word were assumed to be "ON." The ON would be the initial wheel setting when the first character is enciphered. The enciphering equations hold:

$$C = K_r \oplus P$$
$$P = K_r \oplus Z.$$

The first characters of the ciphertext are, 4, 6, Z, 7, G..., shown in column 1 of Table B.3 With ON set on the machine the outputs of Wheel $K_9 = 1$ and $K_{10} = 0$. $K_9 \oplus K_{10} = K_{r5} = 1$ is shown in column 5 of the table.* When the output of K_{r5} is Xor with the fifth bit of the ciphertext codes, a tentative plaintext for the fifth bit is shown in the sixth column $P_5 = 0$.

Wheels 9 and 10 were stepped and the values of P_5 were successively found and recorded. The sequence is, 0 0 0 1 1 etc.

---

* Wheel 9 was indexed by O and wheel 10 was indexed by N. These two wheels form the key bit for channel 5 of the plaintext.

Table B.3 First Test

Ciphertext, C	Codes, Z	K_9	K_{10}	K_{r5}	P_5
4	11111	1	0	1	0
6	00000	0	0	0	0
Z	10001	1	0	1	0
7	00010	0	1	1	1
G	01011	1	1	0	1
E	10000	0	1	1	1
N	00110	1	1	0	0
S	10100	0	1	1	1
6	00000	1	1	0	0
P	01101	0	0	0	1
K	11110	1	0	1	1
M	00111	0	0	0	1
I	01100	1	0	1	1
D	10010	0	0	0	0
Y	10101	1	1	0	1

This process was continued for 60 characters of the ciphertext.* At this point, the 1s and 0s were counted for the fifth bit position, P_5, and it was found that there were 30 1s and 30 0s. This was a clear indication that the starting position ON was incorrect. Table B.2 shows that, for channel 5, 0.674 of the bits should be 0s, not 6/15 = 0.4.†

A number of other starting positions for wheels 9 and 10, the key for the fifth channel position, were tried with the results shown in Table B.4.

Table B.4 Test Results

Cribs	0s	1s	Total	% 0s
ON	30	30	60	50
NT	57	93	150	38
ST	64	56	120	53
NS	28	32	60	47
AT	46	44	90	51
CE	28	32	60	47
LE	46	44	90	51
SE	27	33	60	45
ES	105	45	150	70

With 70% 0s, ES was an excellent candidate for the last two characters of the key word.

The other wheels were examined in pairs. By making further guesses as to the other key characters the key word PRIORITIES was discovered. The ease with which this ciphertext message was found shows the security problem of using only common 10-character words for the key.

* Not all of the 60 are shown in Table B.3.

† However, Kullback tells the humorous story of how some guessed that ON were the last letters of WASHINGTON, a crib that Friedman first rejected as being unworthy of Col. Hitt.

Solution of a Message Set Without the First Message

The other four test messages consisted of a series of messages where the first message of the series was not provided. It was common practice to connect several messages in a string with only one key, that of the first message. The key was allowed to run as each of the connected messages was enciphered.* Under such circumstances, the first few messages were sometimes lost by the intercept operators and the key was obscure. This set of messages was planned to test the security of the system under these circumstances.

The test set consisted of the third, fourth, and fifth messages with the first two missing. The solution of this problem was found because the endings of each message were the same in the first test case. What was not known was how the endings could be identified when the messages were received by the intercept station.

The team had four cribs of six letters to work with (the message endings) and the task of finding the key proceeded as in *Solution Where a Portion of the Plaintext is Known*, above. However, this does not seem as straightforward as the report indicates, as the length of the two missing messages would be required to uniquely identify the common 10 character key.

Comments

In retrospect one can ask if the Hitt cipher machine was given a fair trial. This author thinks it was not. The keying and operating procedures could have been changed to increase the security of the device. Several suggestions come to mind.

First, restricting the key to common English language word of ten characters was a major mistake. The number of possible keys was reduced from 1.4×10^{14} to approximately 10,000 or so. And the keys were open to cribs as shown in *Solution Without Knowledge of Any Plaintext* , above. Cribbing would not be possible with random keys if properly used.

Second, the use of stylized message endings provided made-to-order cribs into the ciphertext. The procedure used by the Department of State should never have been permitted.

Third, the belief that a machine would be captured was too pessimistic. If properly deployed to interior lines and if destruction explosives were used, capture would be unlikely. As noted before, a Lorenz machine was not captured until late in the war. A change to the mechanical design of the machine so that wheels could be interchanged would have mitigated the effect of capture.†

Rowlett writes that Friedman was working at that time on the design of a wired rotor cipher machine, the M-134A.[5] He obviously thought that his design was superior to the Hitt design, even with improvements in keying, and that the Hitt design should not be considered further.

The M-134A, with variations, served the Allies well during WWII. There is no indication that messages enciphered on this machine were ever broken by the Axis powers.

---

* This was a common practice with Lorenz operators.
† The Enigma had interchangeable fixed-wired wheels.

References

[1] Rowlett, F. B., *The Story of Magic*, Aegean Park Press, 1998, pg. 70.
[2] Anonymous, *Principles of Solution of Cryptograms Produced By The I. T. & T Cipher machine*, Technical Paper of the Signal Intelligence Section War Plans and Training Division, GPO, 1934, NARA RG457 Box 745, pg. 1.
[3] (Rowlett, *The Story*, 73).
[4] Kullback, S., *Statistical Methods in Cryptanalysis,* 1935. Now published by Aegean Park Press, 1976. Also found in NARA Item # 1869, Box # CBLI65, ACCN# 4260A.
[5] (Rowlett, *The Story,* 75).

Appendix C

Superimposition or Depth

The Dutch born* cryptanalyst, Aguste Kerckhoffs, provided blazing insight into the problem of deciphering polyalphabetic substitution ciphers.

> "It wants only several messages in the same key. The cryptanalyst must align these one above the other so that letters enciphered with the same keyletter will fall into a single column."[1]

The Kerckhoffs method is now called depth and is defined as "two or more texts enciphered on the same key are said to form a depth."[2] Col. Tiltman employed depth to break into the August 30, 1941 message where two almost identical messages were enciphered with the same key. Likewise, Bill Tutte used depth to unravel the wheel pin patterns of this message. The technique of rectangles discussed in Chapters 5 and 8 is another application of depth. In this use single bits formed from logical operations on the ciphertext messages were stacked in depth.

Because of the strength of the Kerckhoffs' method, the reuse of keys is usually forbidden. However, practical considerations in military situations frequently result in some key reuse and provide an opening to a cryptographer.

The word depth has become a more common term than superimposition in recent years and is the word used in this book. See Kahn for a more complete description of this process.[3]

It can be noted that the German cryptanalysts believed that the only possible solution to Enigma ciphers was superimposition or depth from a number of messages.[4] This danger was appreciated most by the Kriegsmarine, which required that the rotor-starting positions be found in a booklet and communicated to the receiving clerk by an indicator or pointer into the book.†

The German Army depended for a number of years on the sending operator selecting three letters at random for the starting positions of the Enigma rotors. This could lead to penetration by depth. The Poles made statistical tests on Enigma messages and found that there were no identically keyed messages to support a superimposition attack.[5] There is no published information that suggests that depth was ever used by the British to break into the Enigma.

When two equal length messages are enciphered by transposition using the same key, a depth of two, anagramming is usually successful in decipherment. The British Special Operations Executive in WWII used Poem Code so that agents in occupied Europe could remember key words that were used for double transposition encipherment. This system was quite vulnerable to breaking by the Germans on depth.[6]

---

* January 19, 1835 in Nuth, Holland.

† Also the procedure on the Fish links with the replacement of twelve-letter indicators by Q codes, see Chapter 2.

The intercept operators at Knockholt were particularly alert to messages that had the same indicators, revealing depth. These messages were given priority treatment and sent immediately by teletype to GCHQ.

References

[1] Kahn, D., *The Codebreakers*, The Macmillan Company, 1967, pg. 236.
[2] Morgan, G. W. *Theory and Analysis of a Letter-Subtractor Machine,* NARA, RG 457, Box 185, No date, Pg. 2.
[3] Kahn, *Codebreakers*, 440-441).
[4] Kahn, D., *Seizing the Enigma*, Houghton Mifflin Co. Boston, 1991, pg. 40.
[5] (ibid., 52).
[6] Marks, *Between Silk and Cyanide*, Touchstone, New York, 2000.

Appendix D

Double Delta Theory

Background

To satisfy the need to set Lorenz X wheels, Bill Tutte devised the double delta algorithm that is based on four considerations. Considerations 1 & 2 came from the analysis of ciphertext messages intercepted and analyzed by GCHQ. Considerations 3 and 4 were the contribution of Bill Tutte. These four considerations are:

1) There is no statistical information in one channel of the ciphertext
2) There is no statistical information in the delta of one channel of the ciphertext
3) There is statistical information in the Xor of the deltas of two channels of the ciphertext
4) The statistical information in 3) can be used to set the X wheels.

The following discussion is based on contemporary documents [1] and a recent derivation of the equations that are the basis of wheel setting.[2] It is not revealed in the contemporary documents whether or not the Germans performed this analysis. I tend to believe that GCHQ mathematicians did this analysis after the fact in order to satisfy themselves that they understood the reason why, after the message of August 30, 1941, the keying seemed to be random for single channels.

First Consideration

Chapter 9 described how the Germans selected the pin patterns on the X and S wheels so that a single channel was monographically flat. That is, there are approximately an equal number of 1s and 0s on the X and S wheels. Extensive analysis of ciphertext messages confirmed the success of the German selection procedure

Second Consideration

The Germans took steps to insure that the delta of a single channel of ciphertext had no useful statistical information. This goal was insured by giving the S wheel random pin patterns. The following analysis is based on Carter. [3]

Recall that $\Delta D_i = \Delta P_i \oplus \Delta S'_i$

The task is to find the probability that $\Delta D_i = 0$. This will give a view of the statistics of a single channel of ciphertext. To find this probability note there are two conditions where $\Delta D_i = 0$.

1. $\Delta P_i = 0$ and $\Delta S'_i = 0$

2. $\Delta P_i = 1$ and $\Delta S'_i = 1$

Thus: $P[\Delta D_i = 0] = (P[\Delta P_i = 0] \bullet P[\Delta S'_i = 0]) + ([P[\Delta P_i = 1] \bullet P[\Delta S'_i = 1])$.
We now find the value of each of the four probabilities.

I. Find $P[\Delta S'_i = 1]$

There are two conditions for $\Delta S'_i = 1$:

1) When the *S* wheel move, being driven by the *M* wheels.
2) When $P[\Delta S_i = 1] = 0.5\ (1+\beta_i)$.

The German key designers wanted $P[\Delta S'_i = 1] = 0.5$. Thus each of the two conditions must have probabilities of approximately 0.7; $0.7 \times 0.7 \approx 0.5$.

For the first condition, let P[*S* wheels move] = a.*
And
For the second condition, let $P[\Delta S_i = 1] = 0.5\ (1+\beta_i)$

β_i is approximately a fraction of 1s to the total number of pins of an *S* wheel. The Germans set more than ½ pins with 1s on the *S* wheels. For example, Wheel 1 may have been patterned with 22 1s and 21 0s.[4]
The *S* wheel pattern is “stretched” by the irregular stepping by the motor wheels.

Therefore:

$P[\Delta S'_i = 1] = a\ P[\Delta S_i = 1] = a(0.5\ (1+\beta_i))$

The Germans set $a(1+\beta_i) = 1$
Thus,
$P[\Delta S'_i = 1] = 0.5 \times 1 = 0.5$.

Note, with the pin set on the *M* and *S* wheels such that $a(1+\beta_i) = 1$, then $\beta_i = (1\text{-}a)/\ a$.

II. Find $P[\Delta S'_i = 0]$.

It follows from $P[\Delta S'_i = 1] = 0.5$ that $P[\Delta S'_i = 0] = 0.5$.

III. Find $P[\Delta P_i = 1]$.

From Table 4.2 for channel 1, p = 0.5365. And, for any channel, $p \approx 0.5$. In other words, ΔP_i is random for German plaintext. Thus:

$P[\Delta P_i = 1] = 0.5$.

---

* The movement of the *S* wheels is determined by the pin patterns of the *M* wheels.

IV. It follows from $P[\Delta P_i = 1] = 0.5$ that $P[\Delta P_i = 0] = 0.5$.

The probabilities found above are substituted in equation (1)

$$P(\Delta D_i = 0) = P(\Delta P_i = 0) \bullet P(\Delta S'_i = 0) + P(\Delta P_i = 1) \bullet P(\Delta S'_i = 1).$$
$$= 0.5 \bullet 0.5 + 0.5 \bullet 0.5 = 0.5.$$

In other words, ΔD_i is monographically flat with no useful statistical information in a single channel of ciphertext. The German key designers had produced this result by insuring that the *S* and *M* pin patterns had relatively equal numbers of ones and zeros and met the equality $a(1+\beta_i) = 1$

Third Consideration

Bill Tutte posited that there was statistical information in mod2 addition of pairs of two channels of plaintext deltas. With the encipherment characters *X* and *S* being monographically flat, the deltas of the ciphertext carries the fingerprints of the deltas of two channels of the plaintext. It is worth quoting the comment from Walter Jacobs on the statistics of the plaintext.[5]

> "There is not a single process of this section [referring to the Newmanry] that depends on anything but the statistical characteristics of plain text."

When Table 4.2 ΔP is consulted we see that here is statistical information in the plaintext when channels are considered in pairs. The analysis of Table 4.2 shows that $P[(\Delta P_1 + \Delta P_2) = 0] = 0.614$ and it follows that $P[(\Delta P_1 + \Delta P_2) = 1] = 0.386$. Likewise, for channels 4 and 5 we see that $P[(\Delta P_4 + \Delta P_5) = 0] = 0.5775$ and $P[(\Delta P_4 + \Delta P_5) = 1] = 0.4225$.

Other plaintext channel pairs will show similar shifting of the Xor of two plaintext channels away from 0.5. In other words, the result when the deltas of two channels are Xored, the result is shifted from the expected pure chance value of 0.5.

Fourth Consideration

With the mod2 sum of the deltas of two channels of plaintext showing through the monographically flat encipherment, the ciphertext has a bias at the correct setting point.

Chapter 4 described a rationale for the validity of the Double Delta algorithm. From the theoretical considerations discussed in Chapter 4, it may not be intuitive why the score for a set solution is greater (has more zeros) than that of an incorrectly set solution. Another justification is given below.

Consider the following case of two keytext wheel characters (wheels 1 and 2) and three ciphertext characters (wheels 1 and 2).[*] The alignment shown is that when the encipherment is performed.

---

[*] This analysis assumes, as before, that $\Delta S'$ is zero most of the time.

$$\begin{array}{cccc} X_{1,1} & X_{2,1} & Z_{1,1} & Z_{2,1} \\ X_{1,2} & X_{2,2} & Z_{1,2} & Z_{2,2} \\ & & Z_{1,3} & Z_{2,3} \end{array}$$

When the Key and ciphertext are correctly set, the token for just this portion of the problem is:

$$\text{Set Token} = X_{1,1} \oplus X_{1,2} \oplus X_{2,1} \oplus X_{2,2} \oplus Z_{1,1} \oplus Z_{1,2} \oplus Z_{2,1} \oplus Z_{2,2}$$

In addition, the ciphertext is a function of the plaintext and the key.

$$Z_{1,1} = P_{1,1} \oplus X_{1,1}$$

$$Z_{1,2} = P_{1,2} \oplus X_{1,2}$$

$$Z_{2,1} = P_{2,1} \oplus X_{2,1}$$

$$Z_{2,2} = P_{2,2} \oplus X_{2,2}$$

Substituting in the Set Token equation gives:

$$\begin{aligned} \text{Set Token} = & X_{1,1} \oplus X_{1,2} \oplus X_{2,1} \oplus X_{2,2} \\ & \oplus P_{1,1} \oplus X_{1,1} \oplus P_{1,2} \oplus X_{1,2} \\ & \oplus P_{2,1} \oplus X_{2,1} \oplus P_{2,2} \oplus X_{2,2} \end{aligned}$$

All of the *Xs* cancel*, thus the Set Token is:

$$\text{Set Token} = P_{1,1} \oplus P_{1,2} \oplus P_{2,1} \oplus P_{2,2} = \Delta P_1 \oplus \Delta P_2.$$

In other words, for the set case the token is just the mod2 sum of the four bits in the plaintext. The plaintext shows through the encipherment. And, as stated before, this token is 0 most of the time i.e. 0.614.

What happens when the key and the ciphertext are not correctly set (Not Set)?

$$\begin{array}{cccc} & & Z_{1,1} & Z_{2,1} \\ X_{1,1} & X_{2,1} & Z_{1,2} & Z_{2,2} \\ X_{1,2} & X_{2,2} & Z_{1,3} & Z_{2,3} \end{array}$$

$$\text{Not Set Token} = X_{1,1} \oplus X_{1,2} \oplus X_{2,1} \oplus X_{2,2} \oplus Z_{1,2} \oplus Z_{2,2} \oplus Z_{1,3} \oplus Z_{2,3}$$

* Because in mod2 arithmetic, $\delta \oplus \delta = 0$

And

$$Z_{1,2} = P_{1,2} \oplus X_{1,2}$$

$$Z_{2,2} = P_{2,2} \oplus X_{2,2}$$

$$Z_{1,3} = P_{1,3} \oplus X_{1,3}$$

$$Z_{2,3} = P_{2,3} \oplus X_{2,3}.$$

$$\text{Not Set Token} = X_{1,1} \oplus X_{1,2} \oplus X_{2,1} \oplus X_{2,2} \oplus P_{1,2} \oplus X_{1,2} \oplus P_{2,2} \oplus X_{2,2} \oplus P_{1,3} \oplus X_{1,3} \oplus P_{2,3} \oplus X_{2,3}$$

$$=(P_{1,2} \oplus P_{2,2} \oplus P_{1,3} \oplus P_{2,3}) \oplus (X_{1,3} \oplus X_{2,3} \oplus X_{1,1} \oplus X_{,2,1})$$

In other words, the Not Set Token is the Xor of the Set Token plus the Xor of four X bits. The probability that the Xor of these four bits is equal to 1 is 0.5. Thus there is a bias added to the Not Set Token resulting in a statistical bias toward 0.5 rather than the statistics of the plaintext.

As the zero tokens are counted, the score of zeros will be greater than the score of ones. This is a very small difference between the Set and the Non Set cases, but great enough to find the wheel settings with some degree of success if the sample size is large, i.e. long ciphertext messages.

References

[1] Anonymous, *Report on British Attack on "FISH"*, Communications Intelligence Technical Paper TS 47, Navy Department, Washington D.C., May 1945, NARA RG 457, Box 607, pg. 25.
[2] Carter, F., *Codebreaking with the Colossus Computer*, The Bletchley Park Trust Reports, November 1996, pp.9-10.
[3] (ibid., 9-10).
[4] (ibid., 9-10)
[5] Jacobs, W., *Cryptanalysis of Tunny Cipher devices*, NARA, RG 457, Box 943, 1945. pg. 4.

Appendix E

Algorithm Notation

The GCHQ cryptanalysts devised a notation, or language, which was used to communicate to the Heath Robinson and Colossus operators the requirements for a run. From these requirements, the various tapes, switches and plugs would be set up and the run executed.[1]

The basic Heath Robinson and Colossus function was to count the outcome of logical events; counting events is basic to any statistical analysis. In computer terminology the operation code is COUNT and, as all operations are the same, the operation code is implied.

There are two other components of the notation, what to count and under what conditions, if any, to make the count. In general the deltas of the ciphertext tape Z are being counted. A string of symbols specify the characters and relationships to count are shown in Table E.1.

Table E.1 What to Count

Symbols	Meaning	Notes
3*	Count all occurrences of $\Delta D_3 = 0$	
1+2*	Count all occurrences of $\Delta D_1 \oplus \Delta D_2 = 0$	+ and p are both symbols used for $\oplus$.
$1^x 4$*	Count all occurrences of $\Delta D_1 = 1$ and $\Delta D_4 = 0$	No operator means logical And.
$1^x2^x3*4^x5^x$	Count all occurrences of ΔD = 11011 (5), Figures (UC).	

A second part of the notation indicates the setting of the X wheels involved in the counting process. For example, the count $1^x2^x3*4^x5^x$ for all possible settings or starting positions of the five X wheels would require 1.6×10^{19} cycles through the ΔD tape. What was generally wanted was a subset of all possible initial settings. Thus a designator was added to the count specifications that separate the wheels into two groups: all settings and setting specified.

The designator symbol is /. If there are no specified settings of the X wheels, there was a blank to the right of /. The four examples of Table E.1 are shown with a designator in Table E.2. Note that the various ΔDs on both sides of / participate in the logical event that is counted.

Table E.2, Designator

Symbols	Meaning	Wheel Settings
3*/	Count all occurrences of $\Delta D_3 = 0$	All 29 settings of X_3 are evaluated. Requires 29 passes in the run.
1+2*/	Count all occurrences of $\Delta D_1 \oplus \Delta D_2 = 0$	All 1,271 settings of X_1 and X_2 evaluated. This operation was later called the "Double Delta" algorithm.* Requires 1,271 passes in the run.
$1^x/4*$	Count all occurrences of $\Delta D_1 = 1$ and $\Delta D_4 = 0$	All 41 settings of X_1 are evaluated. X_4 setting is fixed. Requires 41 passes in the run.†
$3*/1^x2^x4^x5^x$	Count all occurrences of $\Delta D = 11011$ (5), Figures (UC).‡	All 29 settings of X_3 are evaluated with fixed settings for X_1, X_2, X_4, and X_5. Requires 29 passes in the run.

It is not known how the run specifications were conveyed to the machine operators; there was probably a form that contained all the information. For example, the operators needed to know the position of the fixed X wheels so that the electronic keytext generators could be positioned before the run.

There is a question about a run specification that does not involve ΔD. For example, how is a run that counts the 1s, say, in one channel of Z specified? Heath Robinson and Colossus could perform this operation, but were non ΔD operations ever required?

References

[1] Anonymous, *Report on British Attack on "FISH"*, Communications Intelligence Technical Paper TS 47, Navy Department, Washington D.C., May 1945, NARA RG 457, Box 607, pp. 23-24, 41- 42.

---

* This is the wheel setting run described in Chapter 4.

† Notice that the symbols to the right of / specify both a ΔD character and an X character.

‡ Recall from Table 4.3 that Figures (UC) is a high frequency character in ΔD. This run is one of the check runs mentioned in Chapter 4.

Appendix F

Glossary and Symbols

Glossary

Analog	A machine performs the function of another machine but not its implementation. Tunny is an analog of Lorenz.
Auto Mode	Punched paper tape with the plaintext is input to the system and punched paper tape is output.
Basic Motor	The M_2 extended by the irregular stepping from M_1
Bulge	Score - Random expected. See Proportional Bulge.
Channel (1-5)	The five channels of the Baudot Code, called Impulses by GCHQ.
Ciphertext	Plaintext after encipherment
Crib	A guessed or inferred possible word of the plaintext.
Cross, X	Binary 1.
Cryptanalysis	1. Methods of breaking ciphers by one without legitimately possessing the method. 2. The solving of cryptograms
Cryptanalyst	A specialist in cryptanalysis. One who breaks messages without knowing the key.
Current traffic	Ciphertext messages that have been received within the last few hours.
De-chi, D	Pseudo plaintext, $X \oplus S'$.
Decipher	To transform ciphertext into plaintext by one legitimately possessing the method.
Depsiing	The process of removing $\Delta S'$ from ΔP
Digraph	Pair of successive characters
Dot	Binary 0.
Dottage (d)	The ratio of the pins set to "one" on a wheel to the total pin positions.
Encipher	To transform plaintext into ciphertext
Fish	1. Name given by the British to the Lorenz machine. 2. Name given by the British to the overall Lorenz system.
GCHQ	The Government Communications Headquarters at Bletchley Park
Hand Mode	The online use of Lorenz where the sending operator keys in the plaintext and the receiving teleprinter prints the plaintext. See Figure 2.4.
Impulse(s)	The name GCHQ gave to the five channels of the Baudot code.
Indicator	The sequence of 12 alphabetic characters that indicate the starting settings of the 12 wheels. Sometime enciphered, sometime not. In Oct 1942 changed to the Q-code system giving a number that was a pointer to a codebook that give the 12-character indicator.
Integration	Finding K_i from ΔK_i
Key	The twelve wheel pin patterns and the settings of the twelve wheels (the indicator).
Keytext	Enciphering stream of key characters produced by the Lorenz machine.
Limitations	Overriding of Si for a step when a previous bit is a 0.
Message Number	A number attached to each message. Called *Spruchnummer.*
Mod2	Modulo 2, Xor, $\oplus$
Newmanry	Section headed by Mr. M.H.A. Newman charged with developing and using machine methods for setting and breaking X wheels. Formed in December 1942.
$P[Q = 0] = y$	The probability that $Q = 0$ is y

Plaintext	Message to be put into secret form by encipherment
Plaintext or in-clear	Messages sent without encipherment.
Proportional Bulge	(Score – Random expected) ÷ Random expected
QEP	A Q code followed with digits that point to a table containing indicator letters or numerals.
Rectangling	The process of finding ΔK_1 and ΔK_2 from Z⊕ of a single cipher message.
Replica	A copy of an objectthat is true to the original implementation. For example, the Colossus built by Tony Sale.
Run	The execution of a procedure on one of the machine aids such as Colossus, Heath Robinson, and Tunny.
S'	The effective or "stretched" pattern of the *S* wheels.
Score	The sum of the zero tokens from one solution of the Double Delta algorithm for one wheel setting.
Simulated Ciphertext Message	Ciphertext message divided into short messages for stacking in depth for rectangling.
SIS	Signal Intelligence Service, U.S. Army.
Slide	1. Insertion of extraneous or the omission of letters from the ciphertext. 2. Letters omitted or interpolated.
Testery	Section headed by Mr. Ralph Tester charged with, 1. Recovery and solution of Key from Depths 2. Psi and motor setting from de-chi by hand or with the help of Dragon. 3. Producing German plaintext from Tunnies.
Token	The 1or 0 result from applying the double delta algorithm to two channels of ciphertext and keytext. Xor of eight binary values.
Total Motor	1. Basic motor further modified by limitations. 2. The effective motor dots from M1 and M2.
Trigger(s)	1. Name given to the electronic key generators of Colossus. 2. Occasionally used to designate stepping switches.
Tunny	1. Name given by the British to their analogue of the Lorenz machine. 2. The traffic on the first discovered radio link between Vienna and Athens. 3. Generic name sometimes given to Fish.
Wheel Breaking	To find the pin pattern of the pinwheels.
Wheel Pattern	The configuration of the 501 pins of the twelve wheels. Called *Grundschlussel* or ground setting by the Germans.
Wheel Setting	1. Initial positions of twelve wheels, unique for each message. Call *Spruchschlussel* or message setting by the Germans. 2. To find the initial positions of the wheels.

Symbols

1. The first subscript is the channel and the second subscript is the character position in a channel.

For example, the symbols for X and Z are:
$X_{\text{channel (1,2,3,4,or5) character(1, 2,...n)}}$ and $Z_{\text{channel (1,2,3,4,or5)character(1, 2,...n)}}$.

2. Δ, the first difference, $\oplus$, of two bits from the same channel and two sequential characters.

For a general Δ value, the sequential character subscripts are implied and dropped. Only the channel subscript is shown.

3. $\oplus$, The mod2 sum, Exclusive Or, Xor.

4. $Z\oplus$, The mod2 sum of four bits of the ciphertext: $\Delta Z_1 \oplus \Delta Z_2$.

5. Φ, The mod2 sum of two ciphertext characters.

6. $P[(\Delta S'_1 \oplus \Delta S'_2) = 0] > 0.5$ is read: the probability that $(\Delta S'_1 \oplus \Delta S'_2) = 0$ is greater than 0.5.

7. X, keytext stream

8. Z, ciphertext stream

9. P, plaintext stream

10. $K = X \oplus S'$, the composite key.

Index

A

B

C

D

E

F

G

H

I

J

K

L

M

N

O

P

Q

R

S

T

U

V

W

X

Y